GW00670975

'I...'

AN ANTHOLOGY OF DIARISTS

'I...'

AN ANTHOLOGY OF DIARISTS

Edited by

BARBARA WILLARD

Illustrated by

JOHN SERGEANT

CHATTO & WINDUS

Published by
Chatto & Windus Ltd
42 William IV Street
London WC2N4DF

*

Clarke, Irwin and Co Ltd
Toronto

ISBN 0 7011 0490 2

Printed in Great Britain by
Cox & Wyman Ltd
London, Reading and Fakenham

CONTENTS

CONTENTS (continued)

About Diaries

NOTHING written on paper is as personal as a diary. Indeed it may be such a secret document that its writer leaves instructions for it to be burnt unread after his death. Lonely people, shy people are able to treat a diary as a confidante, to whom they can pour out without fear of derision all the hopes and sorrows which make up their lives. Such a diary is like a close friend who knows all but tells nothing. The immense *I-ness* of this kind of diary makes each one a finely drawn portrait of its writer. An autobiography is far less to be trusted, for such works are written with publication in mind. Even a letter is written to be shared, and the reader is a part of it before ever he slits the envelope.

Diary is a word that has seen some changes. *Diarium* meant simply a soldier's daily allowance. Later a diary became the daily record kept by sailors. 'In sea-voyages,' according to Francis Bacon, 'when there is nothing to be seen but sea and sky, men make diaries'. And he goes on to claim that men travelling by land have so much to keep them busy that they have no time for writing. That is a statement to be challenged nowadays, but diaries of travels or expeditions are frequently promised publication before they are even begun. Since the author will have his eye on a reading public, the self-portrait may be entirely absent or else a bit distorted by human vanity – though an account of danger, say, written while the experience is still fresh, is likely to give a keen impression of fear, or courage, or resource.

When diaries are called *Journals*, though the word implies the same form, there is sometimes a more portentous air about them, and it may emerge that they are not day-by-day accounts at all, but events recollected. Daniel Defoe's *Journal of the Plague Year* is far more aptly called by its later title – *A History of the Plague Year*; and John Evelyn does at times gather up his memories of weeks or months. Eighteenth-century ladies changed the name again and called their diaries *day-books*, in which they recorded

not only daily events but every kind of household matter —
recipes for preserves and puddings and medicines, and kitchen
accounts. Day-books are sometimes found among collections of
family papers, but infrequently published. Such records, modest
as they seem, are immensely valuable in building up a social
picture of the times in which they were written. They are just as
important to the historian and the sociologist as the enormous
diary of Samuel Pepys. Pepys, indeed, combines the historical
with the trivial to the point of genius, at one moment praising the
charms of some pretty woman seen in the street, at the next
discussing government affairs or giving an eye-witness account of
the Fire of London.

Though men and women must have been writing for their own
personal and private satisfaction ever since paper and ink became
commonplace, it is from the eighteenth century onwards that
diaries see publication. Pepys's diary had to wait until 1825 to be
deciphered and printed; John Evelyn beat him by only a very few
years. The importance of the diary as a record of times past then
came to be recognised, and diaries have been an accepted section
of a serious publisher's list ever since. Nowadays they will cover
practically every interest that can be named. There are diaries of
travel, of mountaineering expeditions, round-the-world voyages,
lonely endeavours; there are war diaries, writers' diaries, diaries
written by diplomats and politicians, released for publication,
perhaps, after a statutory length of time, maybe revealing truths
about public or international affairs that have long been a matter
for speculation.

There are vast numbers of diaries to choose from, so selection
is important. The diarists included in this book are either
English, or they are foreigners writing about England. With the
exception of the first entry, in which the subject is of paramount
interest with the author lagging behind, they have been chosen
because they are self-revealing as well as socially interesting. An
English diarist frequently quoted is Parson James Woodforde,
writing at the turn of the seventeenth and eighteenth centuries —
but his diary offers far less of a self-portrait than those supplied by
the two reverend gentlemen included here, and so Woodforde is
left out. Beatrix Potter wrote a journal, begun when she was

fifteen. It presents a picture of a girl growing up in a particular society in late Victorian times, passionately interested in art, concerned with small animals; but because it ends before her career proper started, the journal seems not to tell us what we most want to know about the creator of Tom Kitten and the rest.

It stands to reason that the most obvious writers of diaries worth reading must be professional authors – they know how to shape their material, how to present it, how to express themselves tersely. It might be possible to fill such a book as this with literary diarists alone. Of the writers treated here in their role of diarist, one, Fanny Burney, is chiefly displayed in her secondary role of attendant on Queen Charlotte, wife of poor mad George III.

The extracts are arranged chronologically and an attempt has been made not to overload one period at the expense of another. By their attitudes, the diarists should give some impression of time and the change in manners over four hundred or so years. Such extracts are only snippets, as small a part of the whole as any little snippet of cloth used for matching. Like the cloth snippet, they give the merest impression of the yards awaiting to be unrolled. If the impression seems a good one, then it will be found well worth while to seek out the rest of the material at its source.

De Maisse: Journal of 1597

In November 1597 Henri IV of France sent his ambassador, the Sieur de Maisse, to Queen Elizabeth I of England. It was a special mission. De Maisse was to discover if the Queen would be willing to join the French king in peace overtures to Spain. It was nine years since the defeat of the Spanish Armada and the war seemed likely to drag on for ever.

De Maisse writes in his Journal a quietly competent account of England and England's queen as he found them at that time. Elizabeth was then sixty-four years old. The extract given here offers a somewhat scarifying account of her appearance and manner, and a shrewd comment on the Earl of Essex who was forever in and out of favour with the Queen.

The De Maisse Journal appeared for the first time in English in 1931, when it was translated and edited by G. B. Harrison and R. A. Jones of London University, and published by The Nonesuch Press.

1597

12th December
I wrote all this morning to France, and after dinner have been to see the Church of Westminster ... At the end of the Church is a Chapel wherein are buried the Kings and Queens of England, a very fair sight and of marvellous workmanship, and one cannot see nor speak of anything fairer, be it for the work within and

without this chapel, or because of these tombs; nor do I think that anywhere in the world can the like be seen, nor one so fairly adorned. They say that this building was made by King Henry the Seventh, and that the stone was brought from the town of Caen in Normandy ...

The same day at my return I went to see the Earl of Essex, whom I had not yet been able to see. According to report he was feigning illness, and had been in disgrace with the Queen since returning from his voyage. The same day he had been recalled by her Majesty and had been to her, whereat everyone rejoiced. He is well loved, especially by the nobility. Amongst the courtiers the Earl of Essex is the chief person in the Realm of England. He is very tall and verging on ruddy; a man of understanding, and speaks French very fairly. He is entirely given over to arms and the war, and is the only man in England who has won any renown thereby. He is on bad terms with the Treasurer (*Lord Burghley*), his son (*Robert Cecil*), and the Admiral (*Lord Howard of Effingham*), and cannot accommodate himself to them, nor even to the Queen. He is entirely his own Councillor ... I believe that, so far as an Englishman can, he covets glory ...

Here De Maisse describes how London is administered and writes of the Tower and the order at Court. He describes the ceremony involved in arranging the Queen's meal table.

When the Queen is served, a great table is set in the Presence Chamber near the Queen's throne. The cloth being laid, a gentleman and a lady come in, walking from the end of the room with the cover, and make three reverences, the one by the door, the next in the middle of the chamber, the third by the table. Then they set down the cover and the lady tries the food. The guards bring in the meat in the same manner; then the lady tries the food with a piece of bread and gives it to the guards; thence the meat, such as the Queen desires, is carried into the Privy Chamber where she dines. Her service is neither very sumptuous nor delicate. The ladies-in-waiting eat in the Hall, where the Guards sit.

14th December

This day, which was Sunday, the Queen had ordained that I should come to her audience, and had sent her coaches and barges for me, but upon the hour of dinner I was countermanded and told that the Queen was ill and indisposed.

15th December

... Today she sent her coaches and one of her own gentlemen servants to conduct me. When I alighted from my coach Monsieur de Mildmay, formerly ambassador in France, came up to me and led me to the Presence Chamber, where the Lord Chamberlain came to seek me as before and conducted me to the Privy Chamber where the Queen was standing by a window. (*De Maisse had seen the Queen once before and had described her face as 'very aged. It is long and thin, and her teeth are very yellow and unequal ... and on the left side less than on the right. Many of them are missing so that one cannot understand her easily when she speaks quickly.'*) She looked in better health than before. She was clad in a dress of black taffeta, bound with gold lace, and like a robe in the Italian fashion with open sleeves and lined with crimson taffeta. She had a petticoat of white damask, girdled, and open in front, as was also her chemise, in such a manner that she often opened this dress and one could see all her belly, and even to her navel. Her head tire was the same as before. She had bracelets of pearl on her hands, six or seven rows of them. On her head tire she wore a coronet of pearls, of which five or six were marvellously fair ... She greeted me with very good cheer and embraced me, and then, having been some three feet from the window, she went and sat down on her chair of state and caused another to be brought to me, taking care to make me cover, which I did. The business that was accomplished is written in my despatch to the King of the 16th of this month ...

She often called herself foolish and old, saying she was sorry to see me there, and that, after having seen so many wise men and great princes, I should at length come to see a poor woman and a foolish. I was not without an answer, telling her the blessings, virtues and perfections that I had heard of her from stranger Princes, but that was nothing compared with what I saw. With that she was well contented, as she is when anyone commends her for her judgment and prudence, and she is very glad to speak slightingly of her intelligence and sway of mind, so that she may give occasion to commend her ... When anyone speaks of her beauty she says that she was never beautiful, although she had that reputation thirty years ago. Nevertheless she speaks of her beauty as often as she can. As for her natural form and proportion, she is very beautiful; and by chance approaching a door and wishing to raise the tapestry that hung before it, she said to me laughing that she was as big as a door, meaning that she was tall.

... I departed from her audience at night, and she retired half dancing to her chamber, where is her spinet which she is content that everyone should see. The Lord Chamberlain conducted me to the door at the entrance of the Presence Chamber, and then Monsieur Mildmay conducted me to my coach.

John Evelyn, 1620–1706

'I WAS born about twenty minutes past two in the morning on Tuesday the 31st, and last, of October Anno 1620.'

This simple statement, so precise and particular, is typical of the style of John Evelyn. It obtains throughout his diary, which is not entirely a day-by-day record – he frequently gathers together small periods of time and events and then quite obviously 'writes them up' in his journal. So that the early part is really an autobiographical sketch of his childhood, written when he was a grown man and busy about his affairs. Evelyn's father was a country gentleman, of Wotton in Surrey. Richard Evelyn was appointed Sheriff of the county – that is, of Surrey and Sussex, for the two counties were jointly administered at that time. He then commanded a train, John Evelyn tells us, of 'an hundred and sixteen servants in liveries, and everyone liveried in green satin doublets'. Green seems a suitable colour for the Evelyn livery, for John Evelyn's strongest claim to distinction is his immense interest in forestry and horticulture. His first published book was called *Sylva; or a Discourse of Forest Trees*. By the time he died at the age of eighty-five, he had written enormously.

Inevitably, John Evelyn must be compared with his contemporary, Samuel Pepys. Evelyn's circumstances were much easier, he had not to watch out for advantages and struggle to establish himself, as Pepys had. Both men married young girls – Evelyn chose his wife when she was only twelve years old and he was twenty-six; Mrs Evelyn had innumerable

B

children, many of whom died, while Mrs Pepys had none at all. Evelyn is an author, while Pepys is a journalist, a reporter, slapdash and magnificently vivid. The immediacy of Pepys's style makes him the better choice for accounts of the Plague and the Fire of London. Evelyn is grave – his portrait shows a solemn man – Pepys bursts with humour; and his heart is far softer than John Evelyn's, who once, in France, went to watch a criminal tortured.

Evelyn was born thirteen years before Pepys and survived him by three. The two men often met, and each mentions the other in his diary. In 1669 Evelyn writes: 'I went this evening to London to take Mr Pepys to my brother, who was now exceedingly afflicted with a stone in the bladder ... to encourage his resolution to go through with the operation.' In his diary Pepys thanks God every year on the anniversary that he himself went through the gruesome business and so saved his life.

Pepys wrote in 1665: 'By water to Deptford and there made a visit to Mr Evelyn ... He read to me ... very much of his discourse, he hath been many years and now is about, about Gardenage, which will be a most noble and pleasant piece.' Pepys kindly allows for 'a little conceitedness' in the older man.

Between them, these two articulate men of the seventeenth century have left an unsurpassable picture of great and small matters of their time. Each mentions being at Court to see plays performed for the King and his ladies – upon whom Samuel Pepys casts a more than interested eye, while John Evelyn looks severely down his longish nose. Evelyn emerges from his journal just as clearly as Pepys from his.

Evelyn was a man of deep and unshakable principles, both religious and political. He was a devoted father, and his anguish when his children die is equalled by his great courage and humility in bearing these miseries as being the will of God.

John Evelyn's Diary

From the outbreak of the Civil War in 1641, Evelyn was much abroad – he had strong Anglican sympathies and his loyalty was to the King. It was not until 1652, five years a married man, that he returned to England and settled at Sayes Court in Deptford, where his family life began. Through all his travels he was making a great study of the gardens that he saw, and he very soon put his experience to practical use:

1652

22nd March

I went with my brother Evelyn to Wotton, to give him what directions I was able about his garden, which he was now desirous to put into some form; but for which he was to remove a mountain overgrown with huge trees and thicket, with a moat within ten yards of the house. This my brother immediately attempted, and that without great cost, for more than a hundred yards south, by digging down the mountain and flinging it into a rapid stream; it not only carried away the sand etc., but filled up the moat, and levelled that noble area, where now the garden and fountain is. The first occasion of my brother making this alteration was my building the little retiring place between the great wood eastward next the meadow, where, some time after my father's death, I made a triangular pond, or little stew, with an artificial rock, after my coming out of Flanders.

29th April

Was that celebrated eclipse of the sun, so much threatened by the astrologers, and which had so exceedingly alarmed the whole nation that hardly any one would work, nor stir out of their houses. So ridiculously were they abused by knavish and ignorant star-gazers!

10th May

Passing by Smithfield, I saw a miserable creature burning, who had murdered her husband. I went to see some workmanship of that admirable artist, Reeves, famous for perspective, and turning curiosities in ivory.

1653

19th February

I planted the orchard at Sayes Court; new moon, west wind.

25th December

Christmas-day. No churches, or public assembly. I was fain to pass the devotions of that blessed day with my family at home.

1654

8th February
Ash-Wednesday. In contradiction to all custom and decency, the usurper, Cromwell, feasted at the Lord Mayor's, riding in triumph through the city.

14th February
I saw a tame lion play familiarly with a lamb; he was a huge beast, and I thrust my hand into his mouth and found his tongue rough like a cat's . . .

11th July (*Evelyn is travelling about England at this time*):
. . . After dinner, I visited that miracle of a youth, Mr Christopher Wren, nephew to the Bishop of Ely . . .

16th July
We went to another uncle and relative of my wife's, Sir John Glanville, a famous lawyer, formerly Speaker of the House of Commons; his seat is at Broad Hinton, where he now lives but in the Gatehouse, his very fair dwelling-house having been burnt by his own hands to prevent the rebels making a garrison of it . . . On the 19th, to Sir Edward Baynton's . . . After dinner, they went to bowls, and, in the meantime, our coachmen were made so exceeding drunk, that in returning home we escaped great dangers . . .

18th August
We went to Beverley (*Yorkshire*), a large town with two stately churches, St John's and St Mary's, not much inferior to the best of our Cathedrals. Here a very old woman showed us the monuments, and, being above 100 years of age, spake the language of Queen Mary's days, in whose time she was born; she was widow of a sexton who had belonged to the church a hundred years.

1655

18th March
Went to London, on purpose to hear that excellent preacher, Dr Jeremy Taylor, on Matt. xiv. 17, showing what were the con-

ditions of obtaining eternal life: also concerning abatements for unavoidable infirmities, how cast on the accounts of the cross. On the 31st I made a visit to Dr Jeremy Taylor, to confer with him about some spiritual matters, using him thence forward as my ghostly father. I beseech God Almighty to make me ever mindful of, and thankful for, His Heavenly assistances.

15th April

I went to see the great ship newly built by the Usurper, Oliver, carrying ninety-six brass-guns, and 1000 tons burden. In the prow was Oliver on horseback, trampling six nations under foot, a Scot, Irishman, Dutchman, Frenchman, Spaniard, and English, as was easily made out by their several habits. A Fame held a laurel over his insulting head; the word, *God with us.*

1656

11th July

Came home (*after a trip into East Anglia*) by Greenwich ferry, where I saw Sir J. Winter's project of charring sea-coal to burn out the sulphur and render it sweet. He did it by burning the coals in such earthen pots as the glass-men melt their metal, so firing them without consuming them, using a bar of iron in each crucible, or pot, which bar has a hook at one end, that so the coals being melted in a furnace with other crude sea-coals under them, may be drawn out of the pots sticking to the iron, whence they are beaten off in great half-exhausted cinders, which being re-kindled, make a clear pleasant chamber-fire, deprived of the sulphur and arsenic malignity. What success it may have, time will discover.

1657

25th March

. . . The Protector Oliver, now affecting kingship, is petitioned to take the title upon him by all his new-made sycophantic lords etc.; but dares not, for fear of the fanatics, not thoroughly purged out of his rebel army.

21st April

... I ... waited on my Lord Hatton, with whom I dined: at my return, I stepped into Bedlam, where I saw several poor miserable creatures in chains; one of them was mad with making verses. I also visited the Charter-house, formerly belonging to the Carthusians, now an old neat fresh solitary college for decayed gentlemen ... I likewise saw Christ-church and Hospital, a very goodly Gothic building; the hall, school, and lodgings in great order for bringing up many hundreds of poor children of both sexes; it is an exemplary charity.

7th June

My fourth son was born, christened George (after my grandfather); Dr Jeremy Taylor officiated in the drawing-room.

18th June

At Greenwich I saw a sort of cat brought from the East Indies, shaped and snouted like the Egyptian racoon, in the body like a monkey and so footed; the ears and tail like a cat, only the tail much longer, and the skin curiously ringed with black and white; with the tail it wound up its body like a serpent, and so got up into trees, and with it would wrap its whole body round. Its hair was woolly like a lamb; it was exceedingly nimble, gentle, and purred as does the cat.

25th December

Evelyn and his wife were in London, invited to Exeter House, where a service was held in the chapel. Suddenly the house was surrounded by soldiers. Some attending the service were arrested, while others were confined in the house for questioning:

In the afternoon came Colonel Whalley, Goffe and others, from Whitehall, to examine us one by one; some they committed to the Marshal, some to prison. When I came before them, they took my name and abode, examined me why, contrary to the ordinance made, that none should any longer observe the superstitious time of the Nativity (so esteemed by them), I durst offend, and particularly be at Common Prayers, which they told me was but the mass in English, and particularly pray for Charles Stuart; for which we had no Scripture. I told them we did not pray for Charles Stuart, but for all Christian Kings, Princes and Governors. They replied, in so doing we prayed for the King of Spain, too, who was their enemy and a Papist, with other frivolous and ensnaring questions, and much threatening; and finding no colour to detain me, they dismissed me with much pity of my ignorance ... So I got home late the next day; blessed be God!

1658

27th January
After six fits of a quartan ague, with which it pleased God to visit him, died my dear son, Richard, to our inexpressible grief and affliction, five years and three days old only, but at that tender age a prodigy for wit and understanding; for beauty of body, a very angel; for endowment of mind, of incredible and rare hopes ... Thou gavest him to us, Thou hast taken him from us, blessed be the name of the Lord! That I had anything acceptable to Thee was from Thy grace alone, since from me he had nothing but sin, but that Thou hast pardoned! blessed be my God for ever, Amen ... Here ends the joy of my life, and for which I go even mourning to the grave.

15th February
The afflicting hand of God being still upon us, it pleased him also to take away from us this morning my youngest son, George, now seven weeks languishing at nurse, breeding teeth, and ending in a dropsy. God's holy will be done. He was buried in Deptford church, the 17th following.

23rd May
... There was now a collection for persecuted and sequestered Ministers of the Church of England, whereof divers are in prison. A sad day! The Church now in dens and caves of the earth.

31st May
I went to visit my Lady Peterborough, whose son, Mr Mordaunt, prisoner in the Tower, was now on his trial, and acquitted but by

one voice; but that holy martyr, Dr Hewit, was condemned to die without law, jury, or justice, but by a mock Council of State, as they called it. A dangerous, treacherous time!

3rd September
Died that arch-rebel, Oliver Cromwell, called Protector.

22nd September
Saw the superb funeral of the Protector. He was carried from Somerset-House in a velvet bed of state, drawn by six horses housed with the same; the pall held by his new Lords; Oliver lying in effigy, in royal robes, and crowned with a crown, sceptre and globe, like a king. The pendants and guidons were carried by the officers of the army; the Imperial banners, achievements etc., by the heralds in their coats; a rich caparisoned horse, embroidered all over with gold; a knight of honour, armed cap-à-pie, and, after all, his guards, soldiers, and innumerable mourners. In this equipage they proceeded to Westminster; but it was the joyfullest funeral I ever saw; but there were none that cried but dogs, which the soldiers hooted away with a barbarous noise, drinking and taking tobacco in the streets as they went . . .

6th December
Now was published my *French Gardener,* the first and best of the kind that introduced the use of the olitory (*kitchen*) garden to any purpose.

1660

This was a year of great delight for John Evelyn and that majority which had tired of the Commonwealth. Annus Mirabilis, the year is named in Evelyn's Diary, the year of the Restoration of the Stuarts to the throne of England:

29th May
This day, his Majesty, Charles the Second, came to London, after a sad and long exile and calamitous suffering both of the King and Church, being seventeen years. This was also his birthday, and with a triumph of above 20,000 horse and foot,

brandishing their swords, and shouting with inexpressible joy; the way strewed with flowers, the bells ringing, the streets hung with tapestry, fountains running with wine; the Mayor, Aldermen, and all the Companies, in their liveries, chains of gold, and banners; Lords and Nobles, clad in cloth of silver, gold and velvet; the windows and balconies, all set with ladies; trumpets, music, and myriads of people flocking, even so far as from Rochester, so as they were seven hours in passing the city, even from two in the afternoon till nine at night. I stood in the Strand and beheld it, and blessed God. And all this was done without one drop of blood shed, and by that very army that rebelled against him: but it was the Lord's doing, for such a restoration was never mentioned in any history, ancient or modern, since the return of the Jews from the Babylonish captivity; nor so joyful a day and so bright ever seen in this nation, this happening when to expect or effect it was past all human policy.

Samuel Pepys did not witness this scene. He had been with those who sailed to Holland to escort the King back to England. He remained off Dover and merely says: 'This day, it is thought, the King do enter the City of London.'
Through his father-in-law, who had been in the King's service during his exile, Evelyn had the entrée to the Court, and was offered various appointments. He was increasingly a busy man. But he had also time to interest himself in more domestic matters, and in the smaller wonders of the day — such as he witnessed at St Margaret's Fair in Southwark:

13th September
I saw in Southwark, at St Margaret's Fair, monkeys and apes dance, and do other feats of activity, on the high rope; they were gallantly clad à la mode, went upright, saluted the company bowing and pulling off their hats, they saluted one another with as good a grace, as if instructed by a dancing-master; they turned heels over head with a basket having eggs in it, without breaking any; also, with lighted candles in their hands, and on their heads, without extinguishing them, and with vessels of water without spilling a drop. I also saw an Italian wench dance, and perform

all the tricks on the high rope, to admiration: all the court went to see her. Likewise, here was a man who took up a piece of iron cannon of about 400 lb. weight with the hair of his head only.

23rd September
In the midst of all this joy and jubilee, the Duke of Gloucester died of the small-pox, in the prime of youth, and a prince of extraordinary hopes. (*All the town went into mourning. Pepys says that he 'brought a pair of short black stockings to wear over a pair of silk ones'.*)

6th October
I paid the great tax of poll-money, levied for disbanding the army, till now kept up. I paid as an Esquire £10, and one shilling for every servant in my house.

11th October
The regicides who sat on the life of our late King, were brought to trial in the Old Bailey, before a commission of Oyer and Terminer.

14th October
Axtall, Carew, Clement, Hacker, Hewson and Peters, were executed.

17th October
Scott, Scroop, Cook and Jones, suffered for reward of their iniquities at Charing Cross, in sight of the place where they put to death their natural prince, and in the presence of the King his son, whom they also sought to kill. I saw not their execution, but met their quarters, mangled and cut, and reeking, as they were brought from the gallows in baskets on the hurdle. Oh, the miraculous providence of God!

29th October
Going to London, my Lord Mayor's show stopped me in Cheapside; one of the pageants presented a great wood, with the royal oak, and history of his Majesty's miraculous escape at Boscobel.

1661

1st May
I went to Hyde Park to take the air, where was his Majesty and an innumerable appearance of gallants and rich coaches, being now a time of universal festivity and joy.

3rd May
I went to see the wonderful engine for weaving silk stockings, said to have been the invention of an Oxford scholar forty years since; and I returned by Fromantil's the famous clock-maker, to see some pendules . . .

20th November
At the Royal Society (*which had been founded in* 1645) Sir William Petty proposed divers things for the improvement of shipping: a versatile keel that should be on hinges, and concerning sheathing ships with thin lead.

26th November
I saw *Hamlet, Prince of Denmark* played; but now the old plays begin to disgust this refined age ... (*Pepys, who went the following night, thought the play 'very well done'.*)

1662

11th January
... I received of Sir Peter Ball, the Queen's attorney, a draught of an Act against the nuisance of the smoke of London, to be reformed by removing several trades which are the cause of it, and endanger the health of the King and his people ...

30th May (*The King had married the Portuguese princess, Catherine of Braganza, on her arrival in England the previous week.*)
The Queen arrived with a train of Portuguese ladies in their monstrous fardingales, or guard-infantes, their complexions olivader and sufficiently unagreable. Her Majesty is the same habit, her fore-top long and turned aside very strangely. She was yet of the handsomest countenance of all the rest, and, though low of stature, prettily shaped, languishing and excellent eyes, her teeth wronging her mouth by sticking a little too far out; for the rest, lovely enough.

8th June
I saw her Majesty at supper privately in her bedchamber.

9th June
I heard the Queen's Portugal music, consisting of pipes, harps, and very ill voices. Hampton Court is as noble and uniform a

pile, and as capacious as any Gothic architecture can have made it. There is an incomparable furniture in it, especially hangings designed by Raphael, very rich with gold; also many rare pictures, especially the Caesarean triumphs of Andrea Mantegna, formerly the Duke of Mantua's; of the tapestries, I believe the world can show nothing nobler of the kind than the stories of Abraham and Tobit. The gallery of horns is very particular for the vast beams of stags, elks, antelopes etc. The Queen's bed was an embroidery of silver on crimson velvet, and cost £8000, being a present made by the States of Holland when his Majesty returned, and had formerly been given by them to our King's sister, the Princess of Orange, and, being bought of her again, was now presented to the King. The great looking-glass and toilet, of beaten and massive gold, was given by the Queen-Mother. The Queen brought over with her from Portugal such Indian cabinets as had never before been seen here. The great hall is a most magnificent room. The chapel-roof excellently fretted and gilt. I was also curious to visit the wardrobe and tents, and other furniture of state. The park, formerly a flat and naked piece of ground, now planted with sweet rows of lime trees; and the canal for water now near perfected; also the hare-park. In the garden is a rich and noble fountain, with Sirens, statues etc., cast in copper, by Fanelli; but no plenty of water. The cradle-work of hornbeam in the garden is, for the perplexed twining of the trees, very observable. There is a parterre which they call Paradise, in which is a pretty banqueting-house set over a cave, or cellar. All these gardens might be exceedingly improved, as being too narrow for such a palace.

1664

26th March
It pleased God to take away my son, Richard, now a month old, yet without any sickness of danger perceivably; we suspected much the nurse had over-lain him; to our extreme sorrow, being now again reduced to one: but God's will be done.

Evelyn continued his active and observant way of life, sitting on Commissions for this and that, welcomed at Court — though conditions there were beginning to trouble him and disillusion had set in — praised for his writings. The Dutch war had broken out most disastrously. He was in charge of prisoners and the wounded, but still found time to describe daily events, concerts, the newly invented harpsichord, an address given at the Royal Society in honour of the distinguished Dr Harvey, and so on. The war is occupying him so much in 1665 that he barely mentions the fact that the prevalence of plague has sent the Court out of London. Then comes the entry:

16th *July*
There died of the plague in London this week 1100; and in the week following, above 2000 . . .

But it is Samuel Pepys who describes this time with far greater vividness and anxiety . . .

Samuel Pepys, 1633–1703

Samuel Pepys started his enormous diary in 1660. He had been born in the reign of Charles I, lived through Cromwell's Commonwealth, was to serve Charles II and James II faithfully and loyally, to see the crowning of William and Mary and to live one year into the long reign of Queen Anne. Though he was the son of a poor man he had useful relations who were better situated, and through them he became a civil servant, rising eventually to be Secretary to the Admiralty. His was an energetic and distinguished career – Member of Parliament, Master of Trinity House, President of the Royal Society. He was a man at once vain and anxious, thrifty enough to seem miserly at times, interested in clothes and food and pretty women, the fond husband of a beautiful wife, but childless. He was a collector, someone said, of experiences. More practically, he was a collector of musical instruments. He could play them all, and he could compose songs, too. As a diarist he is perhaps the most famous of all.

Pepys wrote his diary in shorthand – one good reason for the delay in its publication of well over a hundred years. Early editions were very much cut about, for the editors, with a delicacy they would not be likely to feel today, hesitated to make public so much that was domestic, personal and a little scandalous.

They may have been right, for we can never know why Pepys wrote his diary. Was it for his own comfort and satisfaction, or did he mean it for posterity? When he thought he was losing his sight and decided he must give up journalising, he made an entry which is the only answer we are ever going to get to this question, and a pretty ambiguous answer it is:

And thus ends all that I doubt I shall ever be able to do with my own eyes in the keeping of my Journal, I being not able to it any longer, having done now so long as to undo my eyes almost every time that I take a pen in my hand; and, therefore, resolve, from this time forward, to have it kept by my people in longhand, and must be contented to set down no more than is fit for them and all the world to know; or, if there be anything, I must endeavour to keep a margin in my book open, to add, here and there, a note in shorthand with my own hand.

The fully-dimensioned portrait that spills over every page of Pepys's long diary is about as vivid as any we have of a man of his time. His vanity and his good sense, his scruples and the sheer bounding energy with which he uses every minute of his life are all so clearly expressed that the very tones of his voice seem to come through.

Pepys gives a blow-by-blow account of the progress and horrors of the plague that struck London and other parts of England in 1665, and his description of the Great Fire that followed in September of the next year is probably an even better piece of writing. It is an eye-witness account by a participant rather than a mere observer, vivid and anxious, deeply concerned and practical. Indeed, his reactions are very much the same as those of later Londoners – those who saw the city burning once again in 1940 during Hitler's 'blitz'.

The Diary of Samuel Pepys

1660

January 5th

I dined with Mr Shepley, at my Lord's lodgings, upon his turkey-pie. And so to my office again . . . Then my wife and I, it being a great frost, went to Mrs Jem's, in expectation to eat a sack-posset, but Mr Edward not coming it was put off; and I left my wife playing at cards with her, and went myself to Mr Fage, to consult concerning my nose, who told me it was nothing but cold . . .

6th

This morning Mr Shepley and I did eat our breakfast at Mrs Harper's (my brother John being with me) upon a cold turkey-pie and a goose . . . I took my wife to my cousin, Thomas Pepys, and found them just sat down to dinner, which was very good; only the venison pasty was palpable beef, which was not handsome.

August 19*th* (*Lord's Day*)

. . . Home to dinner, where my wife had on her new petticoat that she bought yesterday, which indeed is a very fine cloth and a fine lace; but that being of light colour, and the lace all silver, it makes no great show.

November 22*nd*

. . . To Mr Fox's where we found Mrs Fox within . . . Mr Fox came in presently, and . . . did take my wife and I to the Queen's presence-chamber . . . The Queen a very little, plain, old woman, and nothing more in her presence in any respect nor garb than any ordinary woman. The Princess of Orange I had often seen before. The Princess Henrietta is very pretty, but much below my expectation; and her dressing of herself with her hair frizzed short up to her ears did make her seem so much less to me. But my wife standing near her with two or three black patches on, and well dressed, did seem to me much handsomer than she . . .

1664

November 13*th* (*Lord's Day*)

This morning to church, where mighty sport to hear our clerk sing out of tune, though his master sits by him that begins and keeps the time aloud for the parish. With my wife within doors, and getting a speech out of *Hamlet*, 'To be or not to be', without book. In the evening to sing psalms, and so to prayers and to bed.

1665

April 3*rd*

To a play at the Duke's, of my Lord Orrery's, called *Mustapha*, which, being not good, made Betterton's part and Ianthe's but ordinary, too. All the pleasure of the play was the King and my Lady Castlemaine were there; and pretty witty Nell . . . which pleased me mightily.

c

1665 was a year of trouble and disaster. The Dutch war waxed and waned, a matter for concern to Pepys, because of his situation at the Admiralty. The appearance of plague in London, however, at first casually noted, became very shortly the more important issue:

June 10th

In the evening home to supper; and there, to my great trouble, hear that the plague is come into the City, though it hath, these three or four weeks since its beginning, been wholly out of the City; but where should it begin but in my good friend and neighbour's, Dr Burnett, in Fenchurch Street; which in both points troubles me greatly.

11th (Lord's Day)

... I saw poor Dr Burnett's door shut; but he hath, I hear, gained great goodwill among his neighbours; for he discovered it himself first, and caused himself to be shut up of his own accord; which was very handsome.

15th

... The town grows very sickly, and people to be afraid of it; there dying this last week of the plague 112, from 43 the week before ...

23rd

... Home by hackney-coach, which is becoming a very dangerous passage nowadays, the sickness increasing mightily.

July 3rd

The season grows so sickly, that it is much to be feared how a man can escape having a share with others in it, for which the good Lord God bless me! or make me fitted to receive it.

22nd

... I met this noon with Dr Burnett, who told me, and I find in the news-books this week that he posted upon the 'Change, that whoever did spread the report that, instead of dying of the plague his servant was by him killed, it was forgery, and showed me the acknowledgement of the master of the pest-house, that his servant died of a bubo on his right groin and two spots on his right thigh, which is the plague . . .

25th
. . . Sad the story of the plague in the City, it growing mightily. . . . The sickness is got into our parish this week, and is got, indeed, everywhere; so that I begin to think of setting things in order, which I pray God to enable me to put, both as to soul and body.

August 8th
To my office a little, and then to the Duke of Albemarle's about some business. The streets empty all the way now, even in London, which is a sad sight. And to Westminster Hall, where talking, hear very sad stories from Mrs Mumford; among others of Michell's son's family. And poor Will, that used to sell us ale at the Hall-door, his wife and three children died, all, I think, in a day . . .

12th
. . . The people die so, that now it seems they are fain to carry the dead to be buried by daylight, the nights not sufficing to do it in. And my Lord Mayor commands people to be within at nine at night all, as they say, that the sick may have liberty to go abroad for air . . .

22nd
. . . I . . . walked to Greenwich, in my way seeing a coffin with a dead body therein, dead of the plague, lying in an open close belonging to Coome farm, which was carried out last night; and the parish have not appointed anybody to bury it, but only set a watch there all day and night, that nobody should go thither or come thence; this disease making us more cruel to one another than we are to dogs . . .

31st

Up; and after putting several things in order to my removal, to Woolwich; the plague having a great increase this week, beyond all expectation, of almost 2000, making the general Bill 7000, odd 100; and the plague above 6000. Thus this month ends with great sadness upon the public, through the greatness of the plague everywhere through the kingdom, almost. Every day sadder and sadder news of its increase. In the City died this week 7496, and of them 6102 of the plague. But it is feared that the true number of the dead this week is near 10,000; partly from the poor that cannot be taken notice of, through the greatness of the number, and partly from the Quakers and others that will not have any bell ring for them ...

September 3rd (Lord's Day)

Up; and put on my coloured silk suit, very fine, and my new periwig, bought a good while since, but durst not wear, because the plague was in Westminster when I bought it; and it is a wonder what will be done, as to periwigs, for nobody will dare to buy any hair, for fear of the infection, that it had been cut off the heads of people dead of the plague ...

October 29th (Lord's Day)

In the street, at Woolwich, did overtake and almost run upon two women crying and carrying a man's coffin between them; I suppose the husband of one of them, which methinks, is a sad thing.

November 9th

... the Bill of Mortality, to all our griefs, is increased 399 this week, and the increase generally through the whole City and suburbs, which makes us all sad.

15th

... The plague, blessed be God! is decreased 400; making the whole this week but 1300 and odd; for which the Lord be praised!

30th

At noon comes Sir Thomas Allen, and I made him dine with me, and very friendly he is, and a good man, I think, but one that professes he loves to get and to save. Great joy we have this week in the weekly Bill, it being 544 in all, and but 333 of the plague; so that we are encouraged to get to London soon as we can. And my father writes as great news of joy to them, that he saw York's waggon go again this week to London, and was full of passengers; and tells me that my aunt Bell hath been dead of the plague these seven weeks.

1666

September 2nd

Some of our maids sitting up late last night to get things ready against our feast today, Jane called us up about three in the morning, to tell us of a great fire they saw in the City. So I rose, and slipped on my nightgown, and went to her window; and thought it to be on the backside of Mark Lane at the farthest; but, being unused to such fires as followed, I thought it far enough off; and so went to bed again, and to sleep.

About seven rose again to dress myself, and there looked out of the window and saw the fire not so much as it was and farther off. So to my closet to set things to rights, after yesterday's cleaning. By and by Jane comes and tells me that she hears that above 300 houses have been burned down tonight by the fire we saw, and that is now burning down all Fish Street, by London Bridge. So I made myself ready presently, and walked to the Tower; and there got up upon one of the high places, Sir J. Robinson's little son going up with me; and there I did see the houses at that end of the bridge all on fire, and an infinite great fire on this and the other side . . . So down, with my heart full of trouble, to the Lieutenant of the Tower, who tells me that it began this morning in the King's baker's house in Pudding Lane, and that it hath burned down St Magnus's Church and most part of Fish Street already. So I down to the waterside, and there got a boat, and through bridge, and there saw a lamentable fire . . . Everybody endeavouring to remove their goods, and flinging into the river, or bringing them into lighters that lay off;

poor people staying in their houses so long as till the fire touched them, and then running into boats, or clambering from one pair of stairs, by the waterside, to another. And, among other things, the poor pigeons, I perceive, were loath to leave their houses, till they burned their wings and fell down. Having stayed, and in an hour's time seen the fire rage every way ... I to Whitehall ... and there up to the King's closet in the Chapel, where people came about me, and I did give them an account dismayed them all, and the word was carried to the King. So I was called for, and did tell the King and the Duke of York what I saw; and that unless his Majesty did command houses to be pulled down nothing could stop the fire. They seemed much troubled, and the King commanded me to go to my Lord Mayor from him, and command him to spare no houses, but to pull down before the fire every way ... At last met my Lord Mayor in Canning Street, like a man spent, with a handkercher about his neck. To the King's message he cried, like a fainting woman, 'Lord! What can I do? I am spent; the people will not obey me. I have been pulling down houses, but the fire overtakes us faster than we can do it.' ... So he left me, and I him, and walked home, and no manner of means used to quench the fire. The houses, too, so very thick thereabouts, and full of matter for burning, as pitch and tar in Thames Street; and warehouses of oil, and wines and brandy, and other things ... And to see the churches all filling with goods by people who themselves should have been quietly there at this time ...

Soon as dined, I ... walked through the City, the streets full of nothing but people and horses and carts loaden with goods, ready to run over one another, and removing goods from one burned house to another. They now removing out of Canning Street, which received goods in the morning, into Lombard Street, and farther ... Met with the King and Duke of York in their barge, and with them to Queenhithe, and there called Sir Richard Browne to them. Their order was only to pull down houses apace, and so below bridge at the waterside; but little was or could be done, the fire coming upon them so fast. Good hopes there was of stopping it at the Three Cranes above, and at Botolf's Wharf below bridge, if care be used; but the wind carries it into

the City, so as we know not by the waterside what it do there.
River full of lighters and boats taking in goods, and good goods
swimming in the water; and only I observed that hardly one
lighter or boat in three that had the goods of a house in it, but
there was a pair of virginals in it ... When we could endure no
more upon the water (*Pepys has met his wife and some friends*) we
to a little alehouse on the Bankside, over against the Three
Cranes, and stayed till it was dark almost, and saw the fire grow;
and as it grew darker, appeared more and more, and in corners
and upon steeples, and between churches and houses, as far as we
could see up the hill of the City, in a most horrid, malicious,
bloody flame, not like the fine flame of an ordinary fire ... We
stayed till, it being darkish, we saw the fire as only one entire arch
of flame from this to the other side of the bridge; and in a bow up
the hill for an arch of above a mile long; it made me weep to see it.
The churches, houses, and all on fire, and flaming at once; and a
horrid noise the flames made, and the cracking of houses at their
ruin. So home with a sad heart, and there find everybody discoursing and lamenting the fire.

3rd
About four o'clock in the morning my Lady Batten sent me a
cart to carry away all my money, and plate, and best things, to
Sir W. Rider's at Bethnal Green. Which I did, riding myself in
my nightgown, in the cart; and, Lord! to see how the streets and
the highways are crowded with people running and riding, and
getting of carts at any rate to fetch away things ... I am eased at
my heart to have my treasure so well secured. Then home, and
with much ado to find a way, nor any sleep all this night to me nor
my poor wife. But then and all this day she and I and all my
people labouring to get away the rest of our things ... and we did
carry them, myself some, over Tower Hill, which was by this time
full of people's goods, bringing their goods thither; and down to
the lighter, which lay at the next quay, above the Tower Dock.
And here was my neighbour's wife, Mrs—, with her pretty child,
and some few of her things, which I did willingly give way to be
saved with mine; but there was no passing with anything through
the postern, the crowd was so great ...

4th

Up by break of day, to get away the remainder of my things; which I did by a lighter at the Iron gate; and my hands so few, it was the afternoon before we could get them all away ... Mrs Turner and her husband supped with my wife and me ... in the office, upon a shoulder of mutton from the cook's without any napkin or anything, in a sad manner, but were merry. Only now and then walking in the garden, and saw how horribly the sky looks, all on a fire in the night, was enough to put us out of our wits; and indeed it was extremely dreadful, for it looks just as if it was at us, and the whole heaven on fire. Now begins the practice of blowing up of houses in Tower Street, those next the Tower, which at first did frighten people more than anything; but it stopped the fire where it was done ...

5th (*with friends to survey the damage*)

... they and I walked into the town and find Fenchurch Street, Gracious (*Gracechurch*) Street, and Lombard Street all in dust. The Exchange a sad sight, nothing standing there of all the statues or pillars, but Sir Thomas Gresham's picture in the corner. (*According to John Evelyn, and more reasonably, Sir Thomas Gresham's statue.*) Into Moorfields (our feet ready to burn, walking through the town among the hot coals), and find that full of people, and poor wretches carrying their goods there, and everybody keeping his goods together by themselves; and a great blessing it is to them that it is fair weather for them to keep abroad night and day; drank there and paid two pence for a plain penny loaf. Thence homeward, having passed through Cheapside and Newgate market, all burned, and seen Anthony Joyce's house on fire; and took up, which I keep by me, a piece of glass of the Mercers' chapel in the street, where much more was, so melted and buckled with the heat of the fire like parchment. I also did see a poor cat taken out of a hole in a chimney, joining to the wall of the Exchange, with the hair all burned off the body, and yet alive. So home at night, and find there good hopes of saving our office; but great endeavours of watching all night, and having men ready; and so we lodged them in the office, and had drink and bread and cheese for them. And I lay down and slept a good night about midnight; though when I rose, I heard that there had been a great alarm of the French and Dutch being risen, which proved nothing. But it is a strange thing to see how long this time did look since Sunday, having been always full of variety of actions, and little sleep, that it looked like a week or more, and I had forgot almost the day of the week.

7th

Up by five o'clock; and, blessed be God! find all well; and by water to Paul's Wharf. Walked thence, and saw all the town burned, and a miserable sight of Paul's church, with all the roofs fallen, and the body of the choir fallen into St Faith's; Paul's school also, Ludgate and Fleet Street; my father's house and the church and a good part of the Temple the like . . . So home and did give orders for my house to be made clean; and then down to Woolwich (*where he had sent his wife*) and there find all well.

15th

. . . home to bed; and find, to my infinite joy, many rooms clean; and myself and wife lie in our own chamber again. But much terrified in the nights nowadays with dreams of fire and falling down of houses.

By the end of that same year, the resilient Samuel Pepys is doing his annual accounts as usual, and finding them on the whole very satisfactory:

December 31st

To my accounts . . . I have spent £1154, which is a sum not fit to be said that ever I should spend in one year. Yet blessed be God! and I pray God make me thankful for it, I do find myself worth in money, all good, above £6200; which is above £1800 more than I was last year . . . One thing I reckon remarkable in my own condition is, that I am come to abound in good plate, so as at all entertainments to be served wholly with silver plates, having two dozen and a half.

His thrift paid a good dividend. His career continued on a fair course, though it was twice threatened with disaster. In an age of shifting loyalties, Pepys found himself once in the Tower, once in prison on charges of corruption. He emerged unscathed. At the time of his death in 1703 *the Crown itself was in debt to him for the sum of* £28,000.

Thomas Turner, 1729–1789

The diary of Thomas Turner of East Hoathly in Sussex first edited by his great-great-granddaughter has often been quoted, but for all that it has led a pretty quiet life since it was printed in 1859 in the *Collections* of the Sussex Archaeological Society. Turner had been dead for sixty years by then. Certainly the diary has no literary merit, and just as certainly its author was a person of little importance in the world. After being a schoolmaster, he took up the more practical business of running the village store, where he seems to have supplied everything from cream of tartar to gold lace and ladies' gowns. Yet this rather unpromising background produces some wonderful diary-writing. Turner really confides in his diary, it is a kind of confessional. Now he is drunk and vowing to be better, now calling on heaven in the most pious terms; shall he really go to the party to celebrate a victory over the French, and assuredly drink too much, or had he better settle down for the evening with a nice book of sermons?

The events Turner records do touch on the outside world, but mostly they are local matters, so slight as to be hardly worth noticing. Out of these small affairs, however, comes a picture of village life in the mid-eighteenth century which is as colourful and as coarse, as boisterous and crowded as any cartoon by Hogarth or Rowlandson.

The Diary of Thomas Turner, 1754–1765

1754

Sunday Feb 8

As I by experience find how much more conducive it is to my health, as well as pleasantness and serenity to my mind, to live in a low, moderate rate of diet, and as I know I shall never be able to comply therewith in so strickt a manner as I should chuse, by the unstable and over-easyness of my temper, I think it therefore fit to draw up Rules of proper Regimen, which I do in the manner and form following, which I hope I shall always have the strictest regard to follow, as I think they are not inconsistent with either religion or morality.

If I am at home, or in company abroad, I will never drink more than four glasses of strong beer: one to toast the King's health, the second to the Royal Family, the third to all friends, and the fourth to the pleasure of the company. If there is either wine or punch, never upon any terms or perswasion to drink more than eight glasses, each glass to hold no more than half a quarter of a pint.

He cannot sustain this idea, and is soon 'a little matter enlivened by liquor, but no wayes drunk'.

1755

30th (June)

This morn my wife and I had words about her going to Lewes tomorrow; Oh, what happiness must there be in the married state, when there is a sincere regard on both sides, and each partie truly satisfied with each other's merits! But it is impossible for tongue or pen to express the uneasiness that attends the contrary . . . I have almost made as it were, a resolution to make a sepperation by settling my affairs and parting in friendship. But is this what I married for? . . .

1756

20th May (Mr Porter is the local parson)

This day I went to Mr Porter's to inform him that the livery lace was not come, when I think Mrs Porter treated me with as much imperious and scornful usage as if she had been what I think she is, more of a Turk and Infidel, than a Christian, and I an abject slave.

22nd (May)

This afternoon there was a funeral sermon for Master Marchant, text – 'Let me die the death of the righteous, and let my last end be like his.' From which words we had a very good sermon, tho' whether it was a funeral sermon they that preached it, and they that pay for it, alone must know; most of us thought it to be a sermon made before the death of Master Marchant.

June 14

Master Durrant and I set out on foot for Lewes, today being the visitation. After church time, I was sworn with many more into office of churchwarden, for which I paid 4s. 6d. After dinner we smoked our pipe. I came home about 10 p.m., thank GOD very safe and sober.

June 21

Attended the funeral of Master Goldsmith at Waldron; this was the merriest funeral that ever I saw, for I can safely say there was no crying.

June 22

This day I saw in the Lewes Journal, that our troops under the command of the Duke of Marlborough had landed at St Maloes, and had burnt or otherwise destroyed 137 vessels of all denominations and after destroying these vessels, he reimbarked his men without loss. This success of our arms must doubtless greatly weaken and distress the French, who I believe are already in a very poor way; but I do not imagine this to be a loss to the French nation adequate to the charge which our nation has been at in setting out and equipping such a fleet as ours; and yet I think it is probably destroying, ruining and taking away the life of many thousands of poor innocent wretches, that perhaps never did, nor thought of doing, any hurt to the British nation.

October 15
. . . My wife having hired a horse of John Watford, about four o'clock we set out on our journey for Hartfield, and as we were riding along near to Hastingford, no more than a foot's pace, the horse stood still, and continued kicking-up until we was both off, in a very dirty hole (but thanks be to God, we received no hurt). My wife was obliged to go in to Hastingford House, to clean herself. My wife and I spent the even at my father Slater's. We dined off some ratios of pork and green sallard.

1757

Jan 28
I went down to Mrs Porter's, and acquainted her I could not get her gown before Monday, who received me with all the affability, courtesy, and good humour immaginable. Oh! what a pleasure it would be to serve them was they always in such a temper; it would even induce me, almost, to forget to take a just profit. In the even I read part of the 'New Whole Duty of Man'.

Feb 2
We supped at Mr Fuller's and spent the evening with a great deal of mirth, till between one and two. Tho. Fuller brought my wife home upon his back. I cannot say I came home sober, though I was far from being bad company. I think we spent the evening with a great deal of pleasure.

Wednesday, 22*nd*
About 4 p.m., I walked down to Whyly. We played at bragg the first part of the even. After ten we went to supper on four boiled chicken, four boiled ducks, minced veal, sausages, cold roast goose, chicken pasty, and ham. Our company, Mr and Mrs Porter, Mr and Mrs Coates, Mrs Atkins, Mrs Hicks, Mr Piper and wife, Joseph Fuller and wife, tho. Fuller and wife, Dame Durrant myself and wife, and Mr French's family.

After supper our behaviour was far from that of serious, harmless mirth; it was downright obstreperious, mixed with a great deal of folly and stupidity. Our diversion was dancing or jumping about, without a violin or any musick, singing of foolish healths, and drinking all the time as fast as it could well be poured down; and the parson of the parish was one among the mixed multitude ... About three o'clock, finding myself to have as much liquor as would do me good, I slipt away unobserved, leaving my wife to make my excuse. Though I was very far from sober, I came home, thank God, very safe and well, without even tumbling; and Mr French's servant brought my wife home, at ten minutes past five.

Thursday February 25 (This must really be the 23rd)
This morning about six o'clock just as my wife was got to bed, we was waked by Mrs Porter, who pretended she wanted some cream of tartar; but as soon as my wife got out of bed she vowed she would come down. She found Mr Porter, Mr Fuller and his wife, with a lighted candle, and part of a bottle of wine and a glass. The next thing was to have me downstairs, which being apprized of, I fastened my door. Up stairs they came, and threatened to break it open; so I ordered the boys to open it, when they poured into my room; and, as modesty forbid me to get out of bed, so I refrained; but their immodesty permitted them to draw me out of bed, as the common phrase is, topsy-turvey; but, however, at the intercession of Mr Porter, they permitted me to put on my —, and, instead of my upper cloaths, they gave me time to put on my wife's petticoats; and in this manner they made me dance, without shoes and stockings, until they had emptied the bottle of wine, and also a bottle of my beer ... About three o'clock in the afternoon, they found their way to their respective homes, beginning to be a little serious, and, in my opinion, ashamed of their stupid enterprise and drunken preambulation ...

1758

Thursday, June 29
This day we had a rejoicing by ringing the bells etc., for a victory gained over the French by Prince Ferdinand of Brunswick, near

the Lower Rhine. Mr Coates gave me an invitation to come down tomorrow night, to see him, and to rejoice on this occasion. I think this is not a proper way of rejoicing, for I doubt there is little thought of returning thanks to Him that gives success in warr.

Poor Turner is very worried about this celebration. And no wonder for they drank 'health and success to his Majesty and the Royal Family, the King of Prussia, Prince Ferdinand of Brunswick, Lord Anson, his Grace the Duke of Newcastle and his Duchess, Lord Abergavenny, Admiral Boscawen, Mr Pelham of Stanmore, the Earl of Ancram, Lord Gage, Marshall Keith, and several more loyall healths.'

Monday Dec 25
This being Christmas Day, myself and wife at church in the morning. We stayed the Communion; my wife gave 6d., but they not asking me I gave nothing. Oh, may we increase in faith and good works, and maintain and keep the good intentions that I hope we have this day taken up.

1759

Wednesday, May 30 (For some time, his wife's health has steadily declined.)
My wife very ill all day. Oh, melancholy time; what will become of me I cannot think! Very little trade, and she always so afflicted with illness; but let me not repine; possibly it is good for us that we have known affliction.

Saturday, July 7
This day received by the post the disagreable news of the French being landed at Dover; but yet I hope it is only a false report, set about by some credilous and fanciful people ... My wife very ill all day, and I think somewhat dangerous.

Mrs Turner died the following year, and her husband, who had so often railed against the miseries of being married to her, was quite desolate. 'In her I have lost a sincere friend, a virtuous wife, a

prudent econimist in her family, and a very valuable companion.'
(*It is not surprising to find the poor old hypocrite drunk once more.*) 'I
am intollerable bad: my conscience tears me in pieces.'

In 1765, Thomas Turner found himself a second wife:

'I have, it's true not married a learned lady, nor is she a gay one;
but I trust she is good-natured, and one that will use her utmost
endeavour to make me happy. As to her fortune, I shall one day
have something considerable, and there seems to be rather a
flowing stream. Well here let us drop the subject, and begin a
new one.'

And at that watershed in his life, the Diary of Thomas Turner ends.

George Macartney

Viscount of Dervock, County Antrim, 1737–1806

By the last part of the eighteenth century trade between England and the East was constantly increasing. The East India Company operated in an ever expanding world. China, however, remained aloof from diplomatic entanglements. Various trade missions had a footing in the country, but since Confucian teaching looked upon trade as a very low business, their dealings were all with Chinese merchants; no higher authority admitted their existence.

In 1792, Lord Macartney, a gentleman of considerable experience in foreign diplomacy, was sent at the head of an Embassy from King George III to the Chinese Emperor Ch'ien Lung. It was a difficult mission, very largely because of the inflexible Court etiquette. All who approached the Emperor must honour him with the *kotow*, a salutation entailing complete abasement and acknowledgement of the Emperor as the supreme lord and ruler over all others in the world. Lord Macartney had somehow to get over this difficulty – the English would *not* kotow. How he managed a painfully diplomatic operation is told with many other things in the Journal of his China embassy.

Lord Macartney's China Journal, 1793–1794

Lord Macartney's Embassy to China embarked at Spithead on 21st September 1792, aboard the Lion, *a man-o'-war, in company with the* Hindostan, *an Indiaman, and the brig* Jackall. *The diary proper does not commence until the 15th June of the following year, by which time they were approaching the mainland of China.*

1793

Saturday, June 15

This day we sailed on board the *Lion* from Tourane Bay, in Cochin China, accompanied by the *Hindostan* and the two little brigs, *Jackall* and *Clarence*.

Thursday, June 20

At six o'clock a.m. we came to an anchor off the Grand Ladrone in eleven fathoms water, within view of several small islands. The city of Macao bearing seven leagues N.W. of our berth. I sent Sir George Staunton, Mr Maxwell and Captain Mackintosh on shore for intelligence. None of the trading-ships of the season being yet arrived, all the gentlemen of the different European factories (*the headquarters where the factors or agents lived*) were still at Macao.

Sunday, June 30

... A Chinese pilot came on board with some of his people, who seemed never to have seen such a ship as the *Lion* before. They examined everything with great curiosity, and observing the Emperor of China's picture in the cabin, immediately fell flat on their faces before it, and kissed the ground several times with great devotion.

Wednesday, July 24

At daybreak saw the land about twelve miles distant from us. It is low, flat and sandy, with a heavy surf beating upon it with great violence. We sounded, and had ground at six and a half fathoms. We suppose ourselves to be ten leagues to the south-east of Tientsin river. It is thought that the coast is laid down in the chart too far to the westward, or that too much breadth is given to the gulf which, by our reckoning, can not be three degrees from east to west.

Thursday, July 25

... It appears that the expectations of the Chinese have been raised very high, by the manner in which the Embassy was announced, of the presents which it is to be accompanied with. When Sir George Staunton was at Macao he found, on conversing with the gentlemen there, that they were conceived to be of immense value, and when he mentioned what they were, it was thought that the Chinese would be much disappointed. From these considerations Mr Browne was induced to add his fine telescope to what we had already brought, and I have this day completed our apparatus with Parker's great lens, which Captain Mackintosh brought out with him on a speculation, and which he has been prevailed upon to part with on very reasonable terms, forgetting all the profit which he had the prospect of deriving from the sale of so valuable and so uncommon an article ... I flatter myself we have no rivalship to apprehend at Pekin from the appearance of any instruments of a similar kind ... (*Such lenses could be up to* 16 *inches in diameter.*)

Wednesday, July 31

The wind blowing all day very strong from the eastward prevented any boats coming from the shore. At noon two Mandarins of high rank attended by seven large junks laden with a variety of provisions for our ships, came alongside. The profusion of these was so great and so much above our wants that we were obliged to decline accepting the larger part of them. I here insert the list:

20 bullocks, 120 sheep, 120 hogs, 100 fowls, 100 ducks, 160 bags of flour, 160 bags of rice, 14 boxes of Tartar bread, 10 chests of tea, 10 chests of small rice, 10 chests of red rice, 10 chests of white rice, 10 chests of tallow candles, 1000 water melons, 3000 musk melons, 22 boxes of dried peaches, 22 boxes of fruit preserved with sugar, 22 boxes of other fruit, 22 boxes of ochras, 22 boxes of other vegetables, 40 baskets of large cucumbers, 1000 squash cucumbers, 40 bundles of vegetables, 20

measures of peas in the pods, 3 baskets of earthenware or coarse porcelain . . .

The two chief Mandarins are called Wang *ta-jen* and Chou *ta-jen*. Wang and Chou are their family names; *ta-jen* is the title annexed to their rank, and signifies Great Man. Wang is a war Mandarin, has a peacock's feather and a red coral flourished button on his cap, which is the second order. Chou, who wears a blue button, which is a degree inferior to the red, is a civilian and a man of letters . . . These two Mandarins seem to be intelligent men, frank and easy in their address, and communicative in their discourse. They sat down to dinner with us, and though at first a little embarrassed by our knives and forks, soon got over the difficulty . . . and they shook hands with us like Englishmen at their going away . . .

Lord Macartney and his people were treated with continuing cordiality. The place enchants him. He quotes Shakespeare — 'Oh, brave new world That has such people in it!' and is filled with increasing hope of a successful Embassy. The birthday celebrations of the Emperor are to be kept at Jehol, and at last the delicate matter of procedure and presentation is broached:

Thursday, August 15
. . . They (*Wang and Chou*) then introduced the subject of the Court ceremonies with a degree of art, address and insinuation that I could not avoid admiring. They began by turning the conversation upon the different modes of dress that prevailed among different nations, and, after pretending to examine ours particularly, seemed to prefer their own, on account of its being loose and free from ligatures, and of its not impeding or obstructing the genuflexions and prostrations which were, they said, customary to be made by all persons whenever the Emperor appeared in public. They therefore apprehended much inconvenience to us from our knee-buckles and garters, and hinted to us that it would be better to disencumber ourselves of them before we should go to Court. I told them they need not be uneasy about that circumstance, as I supposed, whatever ceremonies were usual for the Chinese to perform, the Emperor would prefer my

paying him the same obeisance which I did to my own Sovereign. They said they supposed the ceremonies in both countries must be nearly alike, that the form in China was to kneel down upon both knees, and make nine prostrations or inclinations of the head to the ground, and that it never had been, and never could be, dispensed with. I told them ours was somewhat different, and that though I had the most earnest desire to do everything that might be agreable to the Emperor, my first duty must be to do what might be agreable to my own King; but if they were really in earnest in objecting to my following the etiquette of the English Court, I should deliver to them my reply in writing as soon as I arrived in Pekin. They then talked of the length and dangers of our voyage . . . and that the Emperor did not mean to hunt this autumn as usual, but to remove with his Court very early to Pekin on purpose that we might not be delayed. I told them His Imperial Majesty would judge from the King's letter and from my representations what was expected from me on my return to England, and what time would be sufficient to enable me to transact the business I was charged with, and to describe to my Sovereign the glory and virtues of the Emperor, the power and splendour of his empire, the wisdom of its laws and moral institutes, the fame of all which had already reached to the most distant regions . . . all along, ever since our departure from Tientsin, I have entertained a suspicion, from a variety of hints and circumstances, that the customs and policy of the Chinese would not allow us a very long residence among them . . .

Tuesday, August 16
This day at half after six p.m. we arrived at the suburbs of Tungchow, where (our navigation being now ended) we quitted our yachts and went on shore . . . The most refined politeness and sly good breeding appeared in the behaviour of all those Mandarins with whom we had any connection; but although we found an immediate acquiescence in words with everything we seemed to propose, yet, in fact, some ingenious pretence or plausible objection was usually invented to disappoint us. Thus when we desired to make little excursions from our boats into the towns, or into the country, to visit any object that struck us as we went

along, our wishes were seldom gratified. The refusal, or evasion was, however, attended with so much profession, artifice and compliment that we grew soon reconciled and even amused with it. We have indeed been very narrowly watched, and all our customs, habits and proceedings, even of the most trivial nature, observed with an inquisitiveness and jealousy which surpassed all we had read of in the history of China. But we endeavoured always to put the best face upon everything, and to preserve a perfect serenity of countenance upon all occasions. I therefore shut my eyes upon the flags of our yachts (*that is, Chinese transport*) which were inscribed 'The English Ambassador bringing tribute to the Emperor of China', and have made no complaint of it, reserving myself to notice it if a proper opportunity occurs.

Friday, September 6
... This evening our interpreter amused us with an extract from one of the Tientzin gazettes, which seem to be much on a par with our own newspapers for wit and authenticity. In an account given of the presents said to be brought for the Emperor from England the following articles are mentioned: several dwarfs or little men not twelve inches high, but in form and intellect as perfect as grenadiers; an elephant not larger than a cat, and a horse the size of a mouse; a singing-bird as big as a hen that feeds upon charcoal, and devours usually fifty pounds per day; and, lastly, an enchanted pillow, on which whoever lays his head immediately falls asleep, and if he dreams of any distant place, such as Canton, Formosa, or Europe, is instantly transported thither without the fatigue of travelling. This little anecdote, however ridiculous, I thought would not be fair to leave out of my journal.

After seemingly endless haggling over the forms of Court procedure, Lord Macartney has won the day. The Emperor is at Jehol, where the Embassy will be presented. Lord Macartney enters with the following retinue:

An hundred Mandarins on horseback.
Lieutenant-Colonel Benson.

Four Light Dragoons.
Four Light Dragoons.
Four Light Dragoons.
Lieutenant Parish.
Drum.   Fife.
Four Artillerymen.
Four Artillerymen.
A Corporal of Artillery.
Lieutenant Crewe.
Four Infantry.
Four Infantry.
Four Infantry.
Four Infantry.
A Sergeant of Infantry.
Two Servants ⎫
Two Servants ⎪
Two Servants ⎬ in a rich green and gold livery
Two Servants ⎪
Two Servants ⎭
Two Couriers   ditto
Two Musicians ⎫
Two Musicians ⎬ in a rich green and gold livery
Two Gentlemen of the Embassy ⎫
Two Gentlemen of the Embassy ⎬ in a uniform of scarlet
Two Gentlemen of the Embassy ⎭ embroidered with gold
Lord Macartney   ⎫
Sir George Staunton and son ⎬ in a chariot
A servant in livery behind   ditto

It 'made a very splendid show', his Lordship tells us.

Saturday, September 14
This morning at four o'clock a.m. we set out for the Court under
the convoy of Wang and Chou, and reached it in little more than
an hour . . . Sir George Staunton and I went in palanquins and the
officers and gentlemen of the Embassy on horseback. Over a rich
embroidered velvet I wore the mantle of the Order of the Bath,
with the collar, a diamond badge and a diamond star. Sir George
Staunton was dressed in a rich embroidered velvet also, and,

being a Doctor of Laws in the University of Oxford, wore the habit of his degree, which is of scarlet silk, full and flowing . . .

After a long wait, the Emperor arrives:

He was seated in an open palanquin, carried by sixteen bearers, attended by numbers of officers bearing flags, standards and umbrellas, and as he passed we paid him our compliments by kneeling on one knee, whilst all the Chinese made their usual prostrations. As soon as he had ascended his throne I came to the entrance of the tent, and, holding in both my hands a large gold box enriched with diamonds in which was enclosed the King's letter, I walked deliberately up, and ascending the side-steps of the throne, delivered it into the Emperor's own hands, who, having received it, passed it to the Minister, by whom it was placed on the cushion. He then gave me as the first present from him to His Majesty the *ju-eu-jeu* or *giou-giou*, as the symbol of peace and prosperity, and expressed his hopes that my Sovereign and he should always live in good correspondence and amity. It is a whitish, agate-looking stone about a foot and a half long, curiously carved, and highly prized by the Chinese, but to me it does not appear in itself to be of any great value.

The Emperor then presented me with a *ju-eu-jou* of a greenish-coloured stone of the same emblematic character; at the same time he very graciously received from me a pair of beautiful enamelled watches set with diamonds, which I had prepared in consequence of the information given me, and which, having looked at, he passed to the Minister. Sir George Staunton whom, as he had been appointed Minister Plenipotentiary to act in case of my death or departure, I introduced to him as such, now came forward, and after kneeling upon one knee in the same manner which I had done, presented to him two elegant air-guns, and received from him a *jeu-eu-jou* of greenish stone nearly similar to mine. Other presents were sent at the same time to all the gentlemen of my train. We then descended from the steps of the throne, and sat upon cushions at one of the tables on the Emperor's left hand; and at other tables, according to their different ranks, the chief Tartar Princes and the Mandarins of the Court at the same time took their places, all dressed in the proper robes of their respective ranks. The tables were then uncovered and exhibited a sumptuous banquet . . . The order and regularity in serving and removing the dinner was wonderfully exact, and every function of the ceremony performed with such silence and solemnity as in some measure to resemble the celebration of a religious mystery. The Emperor's tent or pavilion, which is circular, I should calculate to be about twenty-four or twenty-five yards in diameter, and is supported by a number of pillars, either gilded, painted or varnished, according to their distance and position . . . The materials and distribution of the furniture within at once displayed grandeur and elegance. The tapestry, the curtains, the carpets, the lanterns, the fringes, the tassels were disposed with such harmony, the colours so artfully varied, and the light and shades so judiciously managed, that the whole assemblage filled the eye with delight, and diffused over the mind a pleasing serenity and repose undisturbed by glitter or affected embellishments. The commanding feature of the ceremony was that calm dignity, that sober pomp of Asiatic greatness, which European refinements have not yet attained.

I forgot to mention that there were present on this occasion three ambassadors from Tatze or Pegu and six Mohammedan ambassadors from the Kalmucks of the south-west, but their appearance was not very splendid. Neither must I omit that, during the ceremony, which lasted five hours, various entertainments of wrestling, tumbling, wire-dancing, together with dramatic representations, were exhibited opposite to the tent, but at a considerable distance from it.

Thus, then, have I seen 'King Solomon in all his glory'. I use this expression, as the scene recalled perfectly to my memory a puppet show of that name which I recollect to have seen in my childhood, and which made so strong an impression on my mind that I thought it a true representation of the highest pitch of human greatness and felicity.

Though things seemed to go so well, Lord Macartney was unable to fulfil his mission and arrange the establishment of a permanent Embassy in Pekin. He was politely sent on his way, though not before he had seen much of China and written of it at length and with great appreciation of its beauties. Perhaps the increasing comparisons with home scenes suggest that novelty was wearing off and he would be glad enough to see England once again. On the 15th January 1794, he concluded his diary of the trip:

. . . I now close my China Journal, in which I have written down the transactions and occurrences of my Embassy and my travels through this Empire, exactly as they passed and as they struck me at the time . . . Should any accident throw this Journal under the eyes of a stranger unacquainted with me and the country I am now quitting, he might possibly imagine that I had too much indulged myself in local description and political conjecture. But nothing could be more fallacious than to judge of China by any European standard. My sole view has been to present things precisely as they impressed me . . . I regularly took notes and memorandums of the business I was engaged in and the objects I saw, partly to serve for my own use and recollection, and partly to amuse the hours of a tedious and painful employment. But I will not flatter myself that they can be of much advantage or entertainment to others.

Fanny Burney, 1752–1840

Fanny Burney, who was born when George II was king, and who lived on into the days of Queen Victoria, originally addressed her diary to *Nobody* – 'since to Nobody can I be wholly unreserved'. However she soon realized its possibilities and towards the end of her life she indulged in a little personal editing; times had changed and she was much concerned by then with propriety.

Fanny was one of six children. Her father was a church organist and teacher, who removed himself from the obscurity of a country town to the wider promise of London. By his own good energies he achieved a musical doctorate and some fame as the author of a vast study called *A General History of Music*. Fanny was a slow learner and at eight she could not read or write. Once she had learnt she seemed unable to stop, and poured out stories and plays and verse. Her stepmother, without any apparent malice, impressed upon her what a wicked waste of time this was, and how horridly unfeminine. At the age of fifteen Fanny made a bonfire of everything she had written.

She was a literary addict, however, and was bound to express herself. In 1778, ten years after the holocaust, her first novel was published anonymously. It was called *Evelina: or, a Young Lady's Entrance into the World*. The novel made Fanny Burney the acknowledged forerunner of Maria Edgeworth and Jane Austen, though both were far better writers. *Evelina* did not remain anonymous for long. It was Fanny who made her entrance into the world, becoming famous, sought after and the friend of eminent men.

Dr Johnson called her his 'dear little Burney'; David Garrick begged her to write a play for him, promising faithfully to put it on.

Success as a novelist may seem a curious qualification for a place at Court. Fanny Burney was offered, and saw no way of refusing, the position of Assistant Keeper of the Robes to Queen Charlotte, the wife of George III. The diary's insights into the rigours and discomforts of the Court régime make it an important social document. The cold rooms opening out of glacial corridors, the early rising, the sheer hard work, the jealousy and back-biting, the terrible anxiety about the King's recurring bouts of madness – all this makes astonishing reading. Fanny was devoted to the Queen and suffered much in silence for her sake. She ruined her health by those years at Court, but worse than that she lost her inspiration. Nothing she wrote in later years could touch the vitality and humour of *Evelina*. She was forty plus when she married a French *emigré*, General D'Arblay. She had one clever, sickly son who died young. She was in Brussels when the Battle of Waterloo was fought, and something of her old descriptive power returns in those pages. As she grew older she most certainly became a snob and a bore. How fortunate that when she was young she felt the need to confide in her diary. That alone will always keep the old original Fanny sparklingly alive.

Fanny Burney's Diary

1778

January

This year was ushered in by a grand and most important event! At the latter end of January, the literary world was favoured with the first publication of the ingenious, learned and most profound Fanny Burney! I doubt not but this memorable affair will, in future times, mark the period whence chronologers will date the zenith of the polite arts in this island!

This admirable authoress has named her most elaborate performance, *Evelina: or, a Young Lady's Entrance into the World*.

Perhaps this may seem a rather bold attempt and title for a female whose knowledge of the world is very confined, and whose inclinations, as well as situation, incline her to a private and domestic life. All I can urge is, that I have only presumed to trace

the accidents and adventures to which a 'young woman' is liable;
I have not pretended to show the world what it actually *is*, but
what it *appears* to a girl of seventeen: and so far as that, surely any
girl who is past seventeen may safely go?

My little book, I am told, is now at all the circulating libraries.
I have an exceeding odd sensation when I consider that it is now
in the power of *any* and *every* body to read what I so carefully
hoarded even from my best friends, till this last month or two; and
that a work which was so lately lodged, in all privacy, in my bur-
eau, may now be seen by every butcher and baker, cobbler and
tinker, throughout the three kingdoms, for the small tribute of
threepence.

Fanny is taken up by the famous Mrs Thrale, the friend and hostess
of many persons of distinction in the arts. At the Thrales's house in
Streatham, Fanny meets Dr Johnson:

August
... Soon after we were seated, this great man entered. I have so
true a veneration for him, that the very sight of him inspires me
with delight and reverence, notwithstanding the cruel infirmities
to which he is subject; for he has almost perpetual convulsive
movements, either of his hands, lips, feet or knees, and sometimes
all together.

Mrs Thrale introduced me to him, and he took his place. We
had a noble dinner, and a most elegant dessert. Dr Johnson, in
the middle of dinner, asked Mrs Thrale what was in some little
pies that were near him.

'Mutton,' answered she, 'so I don't ask you to eat any, because
I know you despise it.'

'No, madam, no,' cried he; 'I despise nothing that is good of
its sort; but I am too proud now to eat of it. Sitting by Miss
Burney makes me very proud today!'

'Miss Burney,' said Mrs Thrale, laughing, 'you must take
great care of your heart if Dr Johnson attacks it; for I assure you
he is not often successless.'

'What's that you say, madam?' cried he; 'are you making
mischief between the young lady and me already?'

A little while after he drank Miss Thrale's health and mine, he then added:

''Tis a terrible thing that we cannot wish young ladies well without wishing them to become old women!'

1785

Fanny goes to stay at Windsor with a very old friend, Mrs Delaney, and there encounters King George III, who comes to call:

November

... O mercy! thought I, that I were but out of the room! Which way shall I escape? And how pass him unnoticed? There is but one single door, at which he entered, in the room! Everyone scampered out of the way ... and Mrs Delaney advanced to meet his Majesty ... I had now retreated to the wall, and purposed gliding softly, though speedily, out of the room; but before I had taken a single step, the King, in a loud whisper to Mrs Delaney, said: 'Is that Miss Burney?' and on her answering: 'Yes, sir,' he bowed, and with a countenance of the most perfect good humour, came close up to me.

A most profound reverence on my part arrested the progress of my intended retreat.

'How long have you been come back, Miss Burney?'

'Two days, sir.'

Unluckily he did not hear me, and repeated his question; and whether the second time he heard me or not, I don't know ...

1786

Fanny has accepted the position of Assistant Keeper of the Robes to Queen Charlotte. Mrs Schwellenberg is Keeper of the Robes; she is a very disagreeable woman.

Monday, July 24

... I rise at six o'clock, dress in a morning gown and cap, and wait my first summons, which is at all times from seven to near eight, but commonly in the exact half hour between them.

The Queen never sends for me until her hair is dressed. This, in a morning, is always done by her wardrobe woman, Mrs

Thielky, a German, but who speaks English perfectly well.

Mrs Schwellenberg, since the first week, has never come down in a morning at all. The Queen's dress is finished by Mrs Thielky and myself. No maid ever enters the room while the Queen is in it. Mrs Thielky hands the things to me, and I put them on. 'Tis fortunate for me I have not the handing them! I should never know which to take first, embarrassed as I am, and should run a prodigious risk of giving the gown before the hoop, and the fan before the neckerchief.

By eight o'clock, or a little after, for she is exceedingly expeditious, she is dressed. She then goes out to join the King, and be joined by the Princesses, and they all proceed to the King's chapel in the Castle (*Windsor*) to prayers, attended by the governesses of the Princesses, and the King's equerry. Various others at times attend; but only these indispensably.

I then return to my own room to brakfast. I make this meal the most pleasant part of the day; I have a book for my companion and I allow myself an hour for it . . .

At nine o'clock I send off my breakfast things, and relinquish my book, to make serious and steady examination of everything I have upon my hands in the way of business — in which preparations for dress are always included, not for the present day alone, but for the Court days, which require a particular dress; for the next arriving birthday of any of the Royal Family, every one of which requires new apparel; for Kew, where the dress is plainest; and for going on here, where the dress is very pleasant to me, requiring no show nor finery, but merely to be neat, not inelegant, and moderately fashionable.

That over, I have my time at my own disposal till a quarter before twelve, except on Wednesdays and Saturdays, when I have it only to a quarter before eleven . . .

These times mentioned call me to the irksome and quick-returning labours of the toilette. The hour advanced on the Wednesdays and Saturdays is for curling and craping the hair, which it now requires twice a week.

A quarter before one is the usual time for the Queen to begin dressing for the day. Mrs Schwellenberg then constantly attends; so do I; Mrs Thielky, of course, at all times. We help her off with her gown, and on with her powdering things, and then the hairdresser is admitted. She generally reads the newspapers during that operation.

When she observes that I have run to her but half dressed, she constantly gives me leave to return and finish as soon as she is seated. If she is grave, and reads steadily on, she dismisses me, whether I am dressed or not; but at all times she never forgets to send me away while she is powdering, with a consideration not to spoil my clothes, that one would not expect belonged to her high station. Neither does she ever detain me without making a point of reading here and there some little paragraph aloud.

When I return, I finish, if anything is undone, my dress, and then take Baretti's *Dialogues* . . . or some such disjointed matter, for the few minutes that elapse ere I am again summoned.

I find her then always removed to the state dressing-room, if any room in this private mansion can have the epithet of state. There, in a very short time, her dress is finished. She then says she won't detain me, and I hear and see no more of her till bed-time.

It is commonly three o'clock when I am thus set at large. And I have then two hours quite at my own disposal: but in the natural course of things, not a moment after! . . .

At five, we have dinner. Mrs Schwellenberg and I meet in the eating-room. We are commonly tête-a-tête: when there is any-body added, it is from her invitation only. Whatever right my place might afford me of also inviting my friends to the table I have now totally lost, by want of courage and spirits to claim it originally.

When we have dined, we go upstairs to her apartment, which is directly over mine. Here we have coffee till the *terracing* is over; this is at about eight o'clock. Our tête-a-tête then finishes, and we come down again to the eating-room. There the equerry, whoever he is, comes to tea constantly, and with him any gentleman that the King or Queen may have invited for the evening; and when the tea is over he conducts them, and goes himself, to the concert room.

This is commonly about nine o'clock.

From that time, if Mrs Schwellenberg is alone, I never quit

E

her for a minute, till I come to my little supper at near eleven.

Between eleven and twelve my last summons usually takes place, earlier and later occasionally. Twenty minutes is the customary time then spent with the Queen: half an hour, I believe, is seldom exceeded.

I then come back, and after doing whatever I can to forward my dress for the next morning, I go to bed – and to sleep, too, believe me: the early rising, and a long day's attention to new affairs and occupations, cause a fatigue so bodily, that nothing mental stands against it, and to sleep I fall the moment I have put out my candle and laid down my head.

This régime Fanny endured for five years less ten days. She travelled about the country as the Court travelled and shared the anxieties that arose from the state of the King's health. At Kew, in attendance on the Queen as usual, she had an encounter with the poor crazy King which is perhaps the most valuable incident in all her long diary:

1789

Monday, February 2nd
What an adventure had I this morning! one that has occasioned me the severest personal terror I ever experienced in my life.

Sir Lucas Pepys persisting that exercise and air were absolutely necessary to save me from illness, I have continued my walks, varying my gardens from Richmond to Kew, according to the accounts I received of the movements of the King. For this I had her Majesty's permission ...

This morning, when I received my intelligence of the King from Dr John Willis, I begged to know where I might walk in safety? 'In Kew Gardens,' he said, 'as the King would be in Richmond.'

'Should any unfortunate circumstance,' I cried, 'at any time, occasion my being seen by his Majesty, do not mention my name, but let me run off without call or notice.'

This he promised. Everybody, indeed, is ordered to keep out of sight.

... I strolled into the gardens. I had proceeded, in my quick way, nearly half the round, when I suddenly perceived, through some trees, two or three figures ... I tried to look sharp, and in so doing, as they were less shaded, I thought I saw the person of his Majesty!

Alarmed past all possible expression, I waited not to know more, but turning back, ran off with all my might. But what was my terror to hear myself pursued! – to hear the voice of the King himself loudly and hoarsely calling to me: 'Miss Burney! Miss Burney!'

I protest I was ready to die. I knew not in what state he would be at the time; I only knew the orders to keep out of his way were universal; that the Queen would highly disapprove of any un-authorised meeting, and that the very action of my running away might deeply, in his present irritable state, offend him. Neverthe-less, on I ran, too terrified to stop, and in search of some short passage, for the garden is full of little labyrinths, by which I might escape ...

Heavens how I ran! I do not think I should have felt the hot lava from Vesuvius – at least not the hot cinders – had I so run during its eruption. My feet were not sensible that they even touched the ground.

At last the doctors in attendance cause Fanny to stop, and she forces herself to turn and greet the King.

... I fairly think I may reckon it the greatest effort of personal courage I have ever made.

The effort answered: I looked up, and met all his wonted benignity of countenance, though something still of wildness in his eyes. Think, however, of my surprise, to feel him put both his hands round my two shoulders, and then kiss my cheek!

... He now spoke in such terms of his pleasure in seeing me, that I soon lost the whole of my terror; astonishment to find him so nearly well, and gratification to see him so pleased, removed every uneasy feeling, and the joy that succeeded, in my conviction of his recovery, made me ready to throw myself at his feet to express it.

What a conversation followed! When he saw me fearless, he

grew more and more alive, and made me walk close by his side, away from the attendants . . .

So they walk together, the King increasingly excited, until at last the doctors intervene and beg him to calm himself:

The tears stood in his eyes – he wiped them, and Dr Willis again became very anxious. 'Come, sir,' he cried, 'now do you come in and let the lady go on her walk – come now, you have talked a long while – so we'll go in – if your Majesty pleases.'

'No, no!' he cried, 'I want to ask her a few questions; I have lived so long out of the world, I know nothing!'

In 1791, Fanny Burney at last escaped her servitude, with rather too many pious exclamations of regret, it may seem to us now. She was thirty-nine years old, but she was not even halfway through her long life. Her diary, her 'dearest of friends' as she now called it, was to continue for many years more.

William Cobbett, 1762–1835

Cobbett scared crows as a child for his Hampshire farmer father. No doubt his early experiences helped to form his later character – he was known as 'the contentious man'. He suffered neither fools nor injustice gladly. He had a packed life, was a soldier, a reformer, a farmer in America as well as England, a writer, a Member of Parliament, a teacher of English to French refugees, a newspaper man forever in trouble for libel – and such a lover of his own countryside that he almost burst with fury to see it mismanaged. He wrote copious journals of his travels about England – what might nowadays be called a 'fact-finding mission' – and these *Rural Rides* are the work by which he is remembered.

Considering his journals are in the nature of a report rather than a personal diary, it is truly amazing how much of the man appears in their pages. They bristle and bustle with the energy of an enthusiast who never shrinks from proclaiming his precise and loud conclusions about places and people and government. His pages are spattered with italics and exclamation marks. He shouts to us across the dividing years. Splenetic is a good old word for William Cobbett, and he must have been a devil to deal with. He emerges, however, for all his prejudices, as blunt, honest, sturdy, and so English as to present an obvious model for John Bull himself. He chuckles and he roars – and as he does so he gives us what may well be the most vivid picture ever conjured up of the English countryside in the bitter days of the early nineteenth century.

Rural Rides, 1821–1832

October 30 *Tuesday* (*Evening*) (Hampshire)
... The fog prevented me from seeing much of the fields as I came along yesterday; but the fields of swedish turnips that I did see were good; pretty good; though not clean and neat like those in Norfolk. The farmers here, as everywhere else, complain most bitterly; but they hang on, like sailors to the masts or hull of a wreck. They read, you will observe, nothing but the country newspapers; they, of course, know nothing of the *cause* of their 'bad times'. They hope 'the times will mend'. If they quit business, they must sell their stock; and, having thought this worth so much money, they cannot endure the thought of selling for a third of the sum. Thus they hang on; thus the landlords will first turn the farmers' pockets inside out; and then their turn comes. To finish the present farmers will not take long ...

Nov 5 Monday (Hampshire)
A *white frost* this morning. The hills round about beautiful at sun-rise, the rooks making that noise which they always make in winter mornings. The starlings are come in large flocks; and, which is deemed a sign of a hard winter, the fieldfares are come at an early season. The haws are very abundant; which, they say, is another sign of a hard winter. The wheat is high enough here, in some fields, 'to hide a hare', which is, indeed, not saying much for it, as a hare knows how to hide herself upon the bare ground. But it is, in some fields, four inches high, and is green and gay, the colour being finer than that of any grass. – The fuel here is wood. Little coal is brought from Andover. A load of faggots does not cost above 10s. So that, in this respect, the labourers are pretty well off. The wages here, and in Berkshire, about 8s a week; but the farmers talk of lowering them ...

Nov 10 *Saturday night* (Herefordshire)
Went to Hereford this morning. It was market-day. My arrival became known, and, I am sure, I cannot tell how. A sort of *buz*

got about. I could perceive here, as I always have elsewhere, very
ardent friends and very bitter enemies; but all full of curiosity.
One thing could not fail to please me exceedingly; my friends
were *gay* and my enemies *gloomy*; the former smiled, and the latter,
in endeavouring to screw their features into a sneer, could get
them no further than the half sour and half sad; the former
seemed, in their looks to say, 'Here he is', and the latter to res-
pond, 'Yes, G—d— him!'—I went into the market-place, amongst
the farmers, with whom, in general, I was very much pleased. If I
were to live in the county two months, I should be acquainted
with every man of them . . .

1822

Thursday (night) 3 January (Sussex)
Points from a speech made by Cobbett against the Corn Laws, at a
lively meeting at Battle:
I am decidedly of opinion, gentlemen, that a Corn Bill of no
description, no matter what its principles or provisions, can do
either tenant or landlord any good; and I am not less decidedly of
opinion, that though prices are now low, they must, all the present
train of public measures continuing, be yet lower, and continue
lower upon an average of years and of seasons. – As to a Corn
Bill; a law to prohibit or check the importation of human food is a
perfect novelty in our history, and ought, therefore, to be received
and entertained with great suspicion . . . When the present Corn
Bill was passed, I, then a farmer, unable to get my brother
farmers to join me, *petitioned singly* again this Bill; and I stated
to my brother farmers, that such a Bill could do us no good,
while it would not fail to excite against us the ill-will of the other
classes of the community; a thought by no means pleasant. Thus
has it been. The distress of agriculture was considerable in
magnitude then; but what is it now? . . . There appears with some
persons to be a notion, that the importation of corn is a *new*
thing. They seem to forget, that, during the last war, when
agriculture was so *prosperous*, the *ports were always open*; that
prodigious quantities of corn were imported during the war;
that, so far from importation being prohibited, high *premiums*
were given, paid out of the taxes, partly raised upon English

farmers, to induce men to import corn. All this seems to be forgotten as much as if it had never taken place; and now the distress of the English farmer is imputed to a cause which was never before an object of his attention, and a desire is expressed to put an end to a branch of commerce which the nation has always freely carried on ... For these reasons, gentlemen (and to state more would be a waste of your time and an affront to your understandings), I am convinced, that, in the way of the Corn Bill, it is impossible for the parliament to afford you any, even the smallest, portion of relief ... Mr Peel's Bill ... has, in effect, doubled, if not tripled, the real amount of the taxes, and violated all contracts for time; given triple gains to every lender, and placed every borrower in jeopardy.

Tuesday 8 January (Lewes)
Came here today, from home, to see what passes tomorrow at a meeting to be held here of the owners and occupiers of land in the rapes of Lewes and Pevensey. – In quitting the great Wen (*London*) we go through Surrey more than half the way to Lewes. From *Saint George's Fields*, which are now covered with houses, we go, towards Croydon, between rows of houses, nearly half the way, and the whole way is nine miles. There are, erected within these four years, two entire miles of stock-jobbers' houses on this one road, and the work goes on with accelerated force! To be sure; for the taxes being, in fact, tripled by Peel's Bill, the fundlords increase in riches; and their accommodations increase, of course. What an at once horrible and ridiculous thing this country would become, if this thing could go on only for a few years! And these rows of new houses, added to the Wen, are proofs of growing prosperity, are they? These make part of the increased capital of the country, do they? But how is the Wen to be *dispersed?* I know not whether it is to be done by knife or by caustic; but dispersed it must be!

Thursday, January 10 (Brighton)
... Brighton is a very pleasant place. For a *wen* remarkably so! The *Kremlin* (the Royal Pavilion), the very name of which has so long been a subject of laughter all over the country, lies in the

gorge of the valley, and amongst the old houses of the town. The grounds, which cannot, I think, exceed a couple or three acres, are surrounded by a wall neither lofty nor good-looking. Above this rise some trees, bad in sorts, stunted in growth, and dirty with smoke. As to the 'palace' as the Brighton newspapers call it, the apartments appear to be all upon the ground floor; and when you see the thing from a distance, you think you see a parcel of *cradle-spits*, of various dimensions, sticking up out of the mouths of so many enormous squat decanters. Take a square box, the sides of which are three feet and a half, and the height a foot and a half. Take a large Norfolk turnip, cut off the green of the leaves, leave the stalks nine inches long, tie these round with a string three inches from the top, and put the turnip on the middle of the top of the box. Then take four turnips of half the size, treat them in the same way, and put them on the corners of the box. Then take a considerable number of bulbs of the crown-imperial, the narcissus, the hyacinth, the tulip, the crocus, and others; let the leaves of each to have sprouted to about an inch, more or less according to the size of the bulb; put all these, pretty promis-cuously but pretty thickly, on the top of the box. Then stand off and look at your architecture. There! That's '*a Kremlin!*' Only you must cut some church-looking windows in the sides of the box. As to what you ought to put *into* the box, that is a subject far above my cut.

Brighton is naturally a place of resort for *expectants*, and a shifty ugly-looking swarm is, of course, assembled here ... You may always know them by their lank jaws, the stiffeners round their necks, their hidden or *no* shirts, their stays, their false shoulders, hips and haunches, their half-whiskers, and by their skins, colour of veal kidney-suet, warmed a little, and then pow-dered with dirty dust. – These people excepted, the people at Brighton make a very fine figure.

1823

Saturday, 2 *August* (Singleton, Sussex)
Ever since the middle of March, I have been trying remedies for the *hooping-cough*, and have, I believe, tried everything, except riding, wet to the skin, two or three hours amongst the clouds on

the South Downs. This remedy is now under trial ... As I came along between Upwaltham and East Dean, I called to me a young man, who, along with other turnip-hoers, was sitting under the shelter of a hedge at breakfast. He came running to me with his victuals in his hand; and I was glad to see that his food consisted of a good lump of household bread and not a very small piece of *bacon*. I did not envy him his appetite, for I had at that moment a very good one of my own; but I wanted to know the distance I had to go before I should get to a good public house. In parting with him, I said, 'You do get some *bacon*, then?' 'Oh, yes! sir,' said he, and with an emphasis and a swag of the head which seemed to say, 'We *must* and *will* have *that*.' ... What sort of *breakfast* could this man have had in a mass of *cold potatoes*? Could he have *worked*, and worked in the wet, too, with such food? Monstrous! No society ought to exist where the labourers live in a hog-like sort of way.

1825

Wednesday 26 *October* (Thursley, Surrey)
... The great business of life, in the country, appertains, in some way or other to the *game*, and especially at this time of the year. If it were not for the game, a country life would be like an *everlasting honeymoon*, which would, in about half a century, put an end to the human race. In towns, or large villages, people make a shift to find the means of rubbing the rust off from each other by a vast variety of sources of contest. A couple of wives meeting in the street, and giving each other a wry look, or a look not quite civil enough, will, if the parties be hard pushed for a ground of contention, do pretty well. But in the country there is, alas! no such resource ... When I see two men, whether in a market-room, by the way-side, in a parlour, in a church-yard, or even in the church itself, engaged in manifestly deep and most moment-ous discourse, I will, if it be any time between September and February, bet ten to one that it is, in some way or other, about *the game*. The wives and daughters hear so much of it that they inevitably get engaged in the disputes; and thus all are kept in a state of vivid animation ... There is, however, an important distinction to be made between *hunters* (including coursers) and

shooters. The latter are, as far as relates to their exploits, a disagreable class compared with the former; and the reason of this is, their doings are almost wholly their own; while in the case of the others, the achievements are the property of the dogs ... Bring me into a room, with a dozen men in it, who have been sporting all day; or rather let me be in an adjoining room, where I can hear the sound of their voices, without being able to distinguish the words, and I will bet ten to one that I tell whether they be hunters or shooters.

Sunday Noon, 30 *Oct* (Winchester)
... After we came out of the cathedral, Richard said, 'Why, papa, nobody can build such places *now*, can they?' 'No, my dear,' said I. 'That building was made when there were no poor wretches in England called *paupers*; when there were no *poor-rates*; when every labouring man was clothed in good woollen cloth; and when all had a plenty of meat and bread and beer.' This talk lasted us to the inn ...

1826

Wednesday 30 *August* (Salisbury)
... It is manifest enough that the *population* of the valley was, at one time, many times over what it is now; for, in the first place, what were the twenty-nine churches built *for?* ... There are now no less than nine of the parishes, out of the twenty-nine, that have either no parsonage-houses at all, or have such as are in such a state that a parson will not, or cannot, live in them ... Nothing can more clearly show, than this, that all, as far as buildings and population are concerned, has been long upon the decline and decay ... The *stars*, in my map, mark the spots where manor-houses, or gentlemen's mansions, formerly stood, and stood, too, only about sixty years ago. Every parish had its manor-house in the first place; and then there were, down this valley, twenty-one others; so that, in this distance of about thirty miles, there stood fifty mansion-houses. Where are they *now?* I believe there are but eight that are at all worthy of the name of mansion-houses; and even these are but poorly kept up, and, except in two or three instances, are of no benefit to the labouring people; they

employ but few persons; and, in short, do not half supply the place of any eight of the old mansions. All these mansions, all these parsonages, aye, and their goods and furniture, together with the clocks, the brass kettles, the brewing-vessels, the good bedding and good clothes and good furniture, and the stock in pigs, or in money, of the inferior classes, in this series of once populous and gay villages and hamlets; all these have been by the accursed system of taxing and funding and paper-money, by the well-known exactions of the state, and by the not less real, though less generally understood extortions of the *monopolies* arising out of paper-money; all these have been, by these accursed means, conveyed away, out of this valley, to the haunts of the tax-eaters and the monopolisers ...

William Cobbett continued his travels, and his account of those travels, for almost ten years. He never swerved in his opinions, nor hesitated to offer his advice — whether it were welcome or unwelcome. In 1832, *he was in the North, and the final paragraph of that particular journal nicely sums up his attitudes and his robust, pugnacious character. He is addressing a local peer:*

7 *October* (Alnwick, Northumberland)
... It is the drones, and not the bees, that are too numerous; it is the vermin who live upon the taxes, and not those who work to raise them, that we want to get rid of. We are keeping fifty thousand tax-eaters to breed gentlemen and ladies for the industrious and laborious to keep. These are the opinions which I promulgate; and whatsoever your flatterers may say to the contrary, and whatever *feelosofical* stuff Brougham and his rabble of writers may put forth, these opinions of mine will finally prevail. I repeat my anxious wish (I would call it a hope if I could), that your father's resolution may be equal to his sense, and that he will do that which is demanded by the right which the people have to insist upon measures necessary to restore the greatness and happiness of the country; and, if he show a disposition to do this, I should deem myself the most criminal of all mankind, if I were to make use of any influence that I possess to render his undertaking more difficult than it naturally must be; but if he

show not that disposition, it will be my bounden duty to endeavour to drive him from the possession of power; for, be the consequence to individuals what they may, the greatness, the freedom, and the happiness of England must be restored.

Dorothy Wordsworth, 1771–1855

Dorothy Wordsworth kept copious records of several periods of her life, but the undeniable best of her is found in The Grasmere Journals. These she kept at Dove Cottage in the Lake District, where she and her brother William settled in 1800. Dorothy had three brothers, but it was William the poet with whom she had most affinity. She was separated from him for much of a not very happy childhood, but at last they set up house together at Grasmere. In later years, the Wordsworth home was more imposing, for they moved a short way in 1813 to the house called Rydal Mount. At Dove Cottage, however, Dorothy is in her true element.

A poet is unlikely to be an easy brother, but nothing cracked the devotion between these two; and though Dorothy was clearly hard pressed when William married Mary Hutchinson, a friend of their childhood, she welcomed his wife with warmth and generosity. The three lived together harmoniously for years, and Dorothy had great delight from the children of the marriage.

The 'I' of these journals is completely selfless – as modest and unobtrusive as any to be found. Dorothy's brother is the centre of her life, his work all-important, and she not only bakes for him and mends for him but copies out endless poems. The intensity with which she lived in that quiet place is poured into her description of the countryside, her own unsophisticated routine and her keen enjoyment of a host of friends, not only fellow poets like Coleridge and Southey, but innumerable neighbours and visitors.

This was life lived to the full in the simplest possible way. Brother and sister are endlessly active. In all weathers they walk and walk – indeed it becomes quite exhausting to follow them day after day, and even in the middle of the night, climbing far and high over the sensational fell tracks; through Dorothy's eyes we can enjoy a Lake District still utterly lonely and unspoilt. They had to walk several miles even to collect letters, and Dorothy and William wrote and received letters by the score. Dorothy writes of William's struggles with one poem or another, his triumph – and hers – when it goes well. They read together, they translate, they worry over Coleridge's health and do rather poorly with their own.

Both are frequently 'rather ill'. William suffers from 'toothach' and does not sleep; Dorothy has colds and 'headach'. These last were a symptom of the illness that overtook her later in life, and in her last years she suffered considerably. It is interesting to find another of our diarists, Francis Kilvert, visiting Miss Hutchinson, the niece of Wordsworth's wife, Mary. This was in 1871, and he heard much of both Wordsworths. Dorothy, he reports, 'was a great walker in her youth' – and he seems to consider that her later sickness was a result of this indulgence. 'When she was middle-aged and growing elderly she thought nothing of walking from Brinsop into Hereford, six miles and back, if she wanted a thimble.' Kilvert speaks of 'her imbecility', of her 'sad state', but Dorothy Wordsworth's most recent editor, Mary Moorman, in the light of modern knowledge states that she suffered from acute arterio-sclerosis.

It needs no particular insight to learn from the Grasmere Journals of Dorothy Wordsworth how much her poet brother was influenced by her keen observation. The rainbow, the cuckoo, the butterfly, even the daffodils can be found first in Dorothy's prose.

'Wordsworth is always referred to as *the poet* in these parts,' wrote Beatrix Potter, visiting the Lakes in 1885, 'and local tradition says that Dorothy Wordsworth was the greater poet of the two.'

The period in which the journals are being written shows in nothing quite so clearly as in the casually mentioned poverty of country folk. Beggars and destitute children weave in and out of the pages, and though there is some kind concern there is no suggestion of any possible remedy.

The most recent edition of The Grasmere Journals, from which these extracts are taken, is Mary Moorman's. She has gone to great trouble to return to the authentic punctuation and spelling, and to sort out the dating, which earlier editors have found confusing. Especially interesting are her footnotes, not only about these doubtful dates and such particular matters, but about small local things – 'A North Country word for a small stream' explains Dorothy's line 'The little syke murmurs'. And where Dorothy gives common flower names, the editor supplies not only the botanical but often the local name as well. Most interesting of all perhaps, in this edition, are the poems written by Dorothy herself. *A Winter's Ramble in Grasmere Vale* has not been published before and by the time she wrote it she was already a sick woman – but all her love and appreciation of that countryside are in the deceptively simple lines.

The Grasmere Journals, 1800–1803

1800

May 14 1800 (*Wednesday*)
Wm and John set off into Yorkshire (*to visit Mary Hutchinson, John's sister*) after dinner at ½ past 2 o'clock, cold pork in their pockets. I left them at the turning of the Low-wood bay under the trees. My heart was so full that I could hardly speak to W. when I gave him a farewell kiss. I sate a long time upon a stone at the margin of the lake, and after a flood of tears my heart was easier. The lake looked to me I knew not why dull and melancholy, and the weltering on the shores seemed a heavy sound. I walked as long as I could amongst the stones of the shore. The wood rich in flowers. A beautiful yellow, palish yellow flower, that looked thick round and double, and smelt very sweet – I supposed it was a ranunculus – Crowfoot, the grassy-leaved Rabbit-toothed white flower, strawberries, geranium – scentless violet, anemones two kinds, orchises, primroses. The heckberry (*bird-cherry*) very beautiful, the crab coming out as a low shrub. Met a blind man, driving a very large beautiful Bull, and a cow – he walked with two sticks. Came home by Clappersgate . . . I resolved to write a journal of the time till W. and J. return, and I set about keeping my resolve because I will not quarrel with myself, and because I shall give Wm pleasure by it when he comes home again.

Sunday 19*th*
Went to church, slight showers, a cold air. The mountains from this window look much greener and I think the valley is more

green than ever. The corn begins to shew itself. The ashes are still bare. Went part of the way home with Miss Simpson (*a Grasmere neighbour*) . . . A little girl from Coniston came to beg. She had lain out all night – her step-mother had turned her out of doors. Her father could not stay at home 'She flights so'. Walked to Ambleside in the evening round the lake. The post was not arrived so I walked thro' the town, past Mrs Taylor's, and met him. Letters from Coleridge and Cottle (*the publisher of* Lyrical Ballads). John Fisher overtook me on the other side of Rydale. He talked much about the alteration in the times, and observed that in a short time there would be only two ranks of people, the very rich and the very poor, for those who have small estates says he are forced to sell, and all the land goes into one hand. Did not reach home till 10 o'clock.

Saturday May 24th
Walked in the morning to Ambleside. I found a letter from Wm and from Mary Hutchinson and Douglass. Returned on the other side of the lakes – wrote to William after dinner, nailed up the beds, worked in the garden, sate in the evening under the trees. I went to bed soon with a bad head-ach. A fine day.

Saturday (7th June)
A very warm cloudy morning, threatening to rain. I walked up to Mr Simpson's to gather gooseberries – it was a very fine after-noon. Little Tommy (*Simpson*) came down with me, ate goose-berry pudding and drank tea with me. We went up the hill to gather sods and plants and went down to the lakeside and took up orchises etc. I watered the garden and weeded. I did not leave home in the expectation of Wm and John, and sitting at work till after 11 o'clock I heard a foot go to the front of the house, turn round, and open the gate. It was William – After our first joy was over, we got some tea. We did not go to bed till 4 o'clock in the morning so he had an opportunity of seeing our improve-ments. The birds were singing, and all looked fresh, though not day. There was a greyness on earth and sky. We did not rise till near 10 in the morning (*Sunday*). We were busy all day in writing letters to Coleridge, Montagu, Douglass, Richard. Mr and Miss

F

Simpson called in the evening, the little Boy carried our letters to Ambleside. We walked with Mr and Miss S. home, on their return. The evening was cold and I was afraid of the tooth-ach for William. We met John on our return home.

Monday morning (28 *July*)
Received a letter from Coleridge enclosing one from Mr Davy about the Lyrical Ballads. (*First published in* 1798, *but due in a new and extended edition that year*, 1800.) Intensely hot. I made pies in the morning. Wm went into the wood and altered his poems. In the Evening it was so very warm that I was too much tired to walk.

Thursday (31*st*)
All the morning I was busy copying poems. Gathered peas, and in the afternoon Coleridge came, very hot, he brought the 2nd volume of the Anthology. The men went to bathe, and we afterwards sailed down to Loughrigg. Read poems on the water, and let the boat take its own course. We walked a long time upon Loughrigg and returned in the grey twilight. The moon just setting as we reached home.

Saturday 22*nd August*
A very fine morning. Wm was composing all the morning. I shelled peas, gathered beans, and worked in the garden till ½ past 12 then walked with William in the wood. The Gleams of sunshine and the stirring trees and gleaming boughs, cheerful lake, most delightful. After dinner we walked to Ambleside – showery – went to see Mr Partridge's house. Came home by Clappersgate. We had intended going by Rydale woods, but it was cold – I was not well, and tired. Got tea immediately and had a fire. Did not reach home till 7 o'clock – mended stockings – and W. read Peter Bell. He read us the Poem of Joanna beside the Rothay by the roadside.

Friday 10*th October*
In the morning when I arose the mists were hanging over the opposite hills and the tops of the highest hills were covered with

snow. There was a most lovely combination at the head of the vale – of the yellow autumnal hills wrapped in sunshine, and overhung with partial mists, the green and yellow trees and the distant snow-topped mountains. It was a most heavenly morning. The Cockermouth traveller came with thread hardware mustard etc. She is very healthy; has travelled over the mountains these thirty years. She does not mind the storms if she can keep her goods dry. Her husband will not travel with an ass, because it is the tramper's badge – she would have one to relieve her from the weary load. She was going to Ulverston and was to return to Ambleside Fair . . .

Friday 24th
A very fine morning. We walked before Wm began to work to the top of the Rydale hill. He was afterwards only partly successful in composition. (*This refers to his long poem,* Michael, *which took several weeks to complete.*) After dinner we walked round Rydale Lake, rich, calm, streaked, very beautiful . . .

Saturday (25th)
A very rainy day. Wm again unsuccessful . . .

Sunday (26th)
. . . Wm composed a good deal – in the morning . . .

28th October, Monday (Here D. W.'s dates are one day ahead of the actual ones, until the following Wednesday, 29th October, hence the two entries with that date.)
. . . Wm could not compose much fatigued with altering.

Tuesday 29th
A very rainy night. I was baking bread in the morning and made a giblet pie . . . Wm looked very well . . .

Wednesday (29th)
William working at his poem all the morning . . .

Monday (24th November)
... A sharp cold night with sleet and snow. I had the tooth-ach in the night. Took Laudanum.

Tuesday (25th)
Very ill – in bed all day – better in the Evening – read Tom Jones – very sleepy slept all night.

Thursday 27th November
Wrote to Tom Hutchinson to desire him to bring Mary with him from Stockton ...

Friday (28th)
Coleridge walked over. Miss Simpson drank tea with us. William walked home with her. Coleridge was very unwell. He went to bed before Wm's return. Great boils upon his neck.

Friday Morning (5th December)
Terribly cold and rainy. Coleridge and Wm set forward towards Keswick but the wind in Coleridge's eyes made him turn back. Sara and I had a grand bread and cake baking. We were very merry in the evening but grew sleepy soon though we did not go to bed till 12 o'clock.

1801

Friday 16th October
Tom Hutchinson came. It rained almost all day. Coleridge poorly.

Saturday 17th
We walked into Easedale. Coleridge poorly after dinner.

Sunday 18th
I have forgotten.

Monday 16th November
A very dankish misty wettish morning. Mary (*Hutchinson*) and Molly ironed all day. I made bread and called at Mr Olliff's –

Mrs O. at home – the prospect soft from the windows. Mrs O. observed that it was beautiful *even* in winter! The Luffs passed us. We walked backwards and forwards in the Church field. Wm somewhat weakish, but on the whole pretty well – he is now at 7 o'clock reading Spenser. Mary is writing beside me. The little syke (*stream*) murmurs. We are quiet and happy . . . I am going to write to Coleridge and Sara . . .

Tuesday 24th
. . . As we were going along we were stopped at once, at the distance perhaps of 50 yards from our favourite Birch tree. It was yielding to the gusty wind with all its tender twigs, the sun shone upon it and it glanced in the wind like a flying sunshiny shower. It was a tree in shape with stem and branches but it was like a Spirit of water. The sun went in and it resumed its purplish appearance the twigs still yielding to the wind but not so visibly to us. The other Birch trees that were near it looked bright and cheerful, but it was a creature by its own self among them . . . We went through the wood . . . There was a rainbow which spanned the lake from the Island house to the foot of Bainriggs. The village looked populous and beautiful. Catkins are coming out palm trees budding – the alder with its plumb coloured buds. We came home over the stepping stones. The Lake was foamy with white waves . . . In speaking of our walk on Sunday Evening the 22nd November I forgot to notice one most impressive sight. It was the moon and the moonlight seen through hurrying driving clouds immediately behind the Stone man upon the top of the hill on the Forest side. Every tooth and every edge of Rock was visible, and the Man stood like a Giant watching from the Roof of a lofty castle. The hill seemed perpendicular from the darkness below it. It was a sight that I could call to mind at any time it was so distinct.

1802

Tuesday 26th January
A dull morning. I have employed myself in writing this journal and reading newspapers till now (½ past 1 o'clock) we are going

to walk, and I am ready and waiting by the kitchen for Wm. We set forward, intending to go into Easedale but the wind being rather loudish, and blowing down Easedale we turned under Silver How for a sheltered walk. We went a little beyond the Wyke then up to John's Grove, where the storm of Thursday has made sad ravages. Two of the finest trees are uprooted one lying with the turf about its root as if the whole together had been pared by a knife. The other is a larch. Several others are blown aside, one is snapped in two. We gathered together a faggot. William had tired himself with working – he resolved to do better. We received a letter from Mary by Fletcher with an account of C's arrival in London. I wrote to Mary before bedtime. We sate nicely together and talked by the fire till we were both tired, for Wm wrote out part of his poem and endeavoured to alter it, and so made himself ill. I copied out the rest for him. We went late to bed. Wm wrote to Annette. (*Wordsworth had travelled in France some years before, and had met and loved Annette Vallon. They had a daughter, Caroline, born in* 1792.)

Friday 12*th February*
A very fine bright, clear, hard frost. William working again. I recopied the Pedlar, but poor William all the time at work ... Just at the closing in of the Day I heard a cart pass the door, and at the same time the dismal sound of a crying Infant. I went to the window and had light enough to see that a man was driving a cart which seemed not to be very full, and that a woman with an infant in her arms was following close behind and a dog close to her. It was a wild and melancholy sight.

Monday 15*th February*
I was starching small linen all the morning. It snowed a good deal and was terribly cold. After dinner it was fair, but I was obliged to run all the way to the foot of the White Moss to get the least bit of warmth into me. I found a letter from C. – he was much better – this was very satisfactory but his letter was not an answer to William's which I had expected. A letter from Annette. I got tea when I reached home and then set on to reading German. I wrote part of a letter to Coleridge, went late to bed and slept badly.

A friend relates an incident which William later made the subject of a poem:

Tuesday 16th

. . . Mr Graham said he wished Wm had been with him the other day – he was riding in a post chaise and he heard a strange cry that he could not understand, the sound continued and he called to the chaise driver to stop. It was a little girl that was crying as if her heart would burst. She had got up behind the chaise and her cloak had been caught by the wheel and was jammed in and it hung there. She was crying after it. Poor thing. Mr Graham took her into the chaise and the cloak was released from the wheel but the child's misery did not cease for her cloak was torn to rags; it had been a miserable cloack before, but she had no other and it was the greatest sorrow that could befal her. Her name was Alice Fell. She had no parents, and belonged to the next Town. At the next Town Mr G. left money with some respectable people in the town to buy her a new cloak.

Wednesday (17th March)

. . . The owls hooted when we sate on the Wall at the foot of White Moss. The sky broke more and more and we saw the moon now and then . . . When we came in sight of our own dear Grasmere, the Vale looked fair and quiet in the moonshine, the Church was there and all the cottages. There were high slow-travelling clouds in the sky that threw large masses of Shade upon some of the Mountains . . . William kindled and began to write the poem. We carried cloaks into the orchard and sate a while there, I left him and he nearly finished the poem. I was tired to death and went to bed before him – he came down to me and read the Poem to me in bed . . .

Thursday (18th)

A very fine morning. The sun shone but it was far colder than yesterday . . . I ate a Beef-steak thinking it would strengthen me so it did, and I went off. I had a very pleasant walk. Rydale vale was full of life and motion. The wind blew briskly and the lake was covered all over with Bright silver waves that were there each

the twinkling of an eye, then others rose up and took their place
as fast as they went away. The Rocks glittered in the sunshine,
the crows and the ravens were busy, and the thrushes and little
Birds sang. I went through the fields, and sate ½ an hour afraid
to pass a Cow. The Cow looked at me and I looked at the Cow
and whenever I stirred the Cow gave over eating . . .

She calls on friends and returns home in the dark:

O the unutterable darkness of the sky and the earth below the
moon! and the glorious brightness of the moon itself! There was
a vivid sparkling streak of light at this end of Rydale water but the
rest was very dark and Loughrigg fell and Silver How were
white and bright as if they were covered with hoar frost. The
moon retired again and appeared and disappeared several times
before I reached home . . . I was tired when I reached home. I
could not sit down to reading and tried to write verses but alas!
I gave up expecting William and went soon to bed . . .

*In August of that year, Dorothy went with William to Calais to
see Annette and Caroline, William's daughter. He had decided to
marry Mary Hutchinson, and so the visit was in the nature of a
farewell.*

We arrived at Calais at 4 o'clock on Sunday morning, the 31st
of July (*it was in fact 1st August*). We stayed in the vessel till
½-past 7, then Wm went for Letters, at about ½ past 8 or 9 we
found out Annette and C. chez Madame Avril dans la Rue de la
Tête d'or. We lodged opposite two Ladies in tolerably decent-
sized rooms but badly furnished and with large store of bad
smells and dirt in the yard, and all about. The weather was very
hot. We walked by the sea-shore almost every evening with
Annette and Caroline or Wm and I alone. I had a bad cold and
could not bathe at first but William did. It was a pretty sight to
see as we walked upon the sands when the tide was low perhaps a
hundred people bathing about ¼ of a mile distant from us, and we
had delightful walks after the heat of the day was passed away –
seeing far off in the west the Coast of England like a cloud

crested with Dover Castle, which was but like the summit of the cloud. The Evening star and the glory of the sky. The Reflections in the water were more beautiful than the sky itself, purple waves brighter than precious stones for ever melting away upon the sands . . .

The decision was now made. The Wordsworths returned to England. Dorothy accepted the inevitable nobly, though like any other sister similarly placed, she must have suffered a considerable emotional upheaval.

On Monday 4th October 1802, my Brother William was married to Mary Hutchinson. I slept a good deal of the night and rose fresh and well in the morning. At a little after 8 o'clock I saw them go down the avenue towards the Church. William had parted from me upstairs. I gave him the wedding ring – with how deep a blessing! I took it from my forefinger where I had worn it the whole of the night before – he slipped it again onto my finger and blessed me fervently. When they were absent my dear little Sara prepared the breakfast. I kept myself as quiet as I could, but when I saw the two men (*John and Tom Hutchinson*) running up the walk, coming to tell us it was over, I could stand it no longer and threw myself on the bed where I lay in stillness, neither hearing or seeing anything, till Sara came upstairs to me and said 'They are coming.' This forced me from the bed where I lay and I moved I knew not how straight forward, faster than my strength could carry me till I met my beloved William and fell upon his bosom. He and John Hutchinson led me to the house and there I stayed to welcome my dear Mary. As soon as we had breakfasted we departed. It rained when we set off. Poor Mary was much agitated when she parted from her Brothers and Sisters and her home . . . (*The journey back to Dove Cottage takes two days.*) It rained very hard when we reached Windermere. We sate in the rain at Wilcock's to change horses, and arrived at Grasmere at about 6 o'clock on Wednesday evening, the 6th of October 1802 . . . I cannot describe what I felt, and our dear Mary's feelings would I dare say not be easy to speak of. We went by candle light into the garden and were astonished at the growth of the Brooms,

Portugal Laurels, etc. etc. etc. The next day, Thursday, we unpacked the Boxes. On Friday 8th we baked Bread, and Mary and
I walked, first upon the Hill side, and then in John's Grove,
then in view of Rydale, the first walk that I had taken with my
Sister.

Gideon Mantell, 1790–1852

The journal begun by Gideon Mantell in 1818 is packed with incident and opinion, with tales of geological discoveries and archaeological theories, together with some detail of medical and surgical practices in the early nineteenth century. What emerges, however, is above all else the portrait of an immensely active, insanely ambitious but disappointed man. Mantell was the son of a shoemaker and became a good and successful doctor with a practice in Lewes, Sussex, where he had been born. His deep interest in geology and his discoveries of the fossil bones of the iguanadon and other giant lizards brought him fame of a kind he had not expected. He was made a Fellow of the Royal Society and was in demand for lectures and the reading of learned papers. Mantell's ambitions were considerable, but they were certainly largely social. He moved to Brighton in order to be near the Royal Pavilion, hoping for exalted patients. But his career as a doctor became swamped by his other activities, his house became a museum, and his marriage quite literally foundered on fossils. He suffered from a spinal condition that caused him a good deal of pain, and perhaps this increased his touchiness, his certainty of being constantly slighted and passed over in favour of inferior men.

The Journal of Gideon Mantell, 1818–1852

The entries for the year 1818 are written in retrospect, so the dating is vague:

August

An immense number of Persons in this Town and neighbourhood are ill with Typhus fever – I have visited upwards of 40 and 50 patients every day for some time; yesterday I visited 64. Our house is like a public office from the continual ingress and egress of persons sending for their medicines. Our little girl Ellen was vaccinated a few days since and went thro' it well. The smallpox is very prevalent – 14 have died with it ... Mrs Woodhouse (my wife's mother) came from London on a visit to our house, she is now dangerously ill with Typhus fever. – Our servant maid is confined to bed with the same complaint ...

September

Received a visit from G. Cumberland Esq. of Bristol – a celebrated geologist – gave him a large box of fossils – and a copy of a Geological Sketch of the Strata of the South Eastern part of Sussex – He considers my collection of Chalk Fossils as one of the most interesting in the kingdom.

December

Mr Moore (*his senior in the practice*) had a most severe fit of Apoplexy; I was with him when it came on and immediately made a large orifice in a vein and took away forty ounces of blood; I then cupped him, had leeches applied etc. He had convulsions repeatedly for three days successively. Dr Blair and Mr Hodson thought his case hopeless ... Upon my return in the evening (*of the third day*) I found Mr Moore in the same state as I had left him: pulse slow and full; breathing sterterous; convulsions every half hour; he was entirely senseless. I resolved to bleed him again as the dernier resort. I took from him 20 ounces; whilst the blood was flowing he muttered out 'better, Mantell, better!' ... Old

Ellis the Bellman ... is crying 'past two o'clock' — I must conclude.

1819

Feb 3
This day I enter on my 30th year! ...

6 *February*
... Gathered primroses near Glyndebourne ...

24
An apprentice of Rider the Blacksmith had his finger shattered to pieces by the fall of a piece of iron: I was obliged to amputate it at the metacarpal joint ...

March 7
This morning I was agreeably surprised at receiving a letter from Thos. Smith Esq., and a Memoir on the poisonous fangs of Serpents, of which he was the Author ...

March 8
... This evening I attended the meeting of the Philosophical Society ...

March 11
Very much fatigued – visited 40 patients.

March 12
In consequence of the illness of my horse I was obliged to visit my country patients on foot. At eight in the morning I set off ... and returned home at Eleven.

14
The new invented Pedestrian Accelerator Hobby-Horse or Velocipede, was exhibited (for the first time in this town) at Mr Bull's warehouse. – It seems likely to be occasionally (but never generally) useful: it is very pleasant and healthy exercise.

March 19

... I am almost fatigued to death. I have been detained with a case of Midwifery two nights and two days ... The Planet Ceres was visible with the Telescope last evening.

1821

December 31

Prevented by the usual occupations of the close of the year from continuing my brief memoranda of passing events. I terminate another year as I did the last; by anticipating moments of leisure and happiness, which in all probability I am destined never to realise. I have made considerable progress in the MS of my intended work on the Geology of Sussex, which I hope to complete in the spring; and the subscribers to it are more numerous and respectable than I could have expected.

1822

31 (*December*)

The past year like its predecessors has fleeted away almost imperceptibly, and I am as far from attaining that eminence in my profession to which I aspire, as at the commencement of it, the publication of my work on the Geology of Sussex, although attended with many flattering circumstances, has not yet procured me that introduction to the first circles in this neighbourhood which I had been led to believe it would have done. In fact I perceive so many chances against my surmounting the prejudice which the humble situation of my family naturally excites in the minds of the great, that I have serious thoughts of trying my fortune either at Brighton or London ...

1825

Dec 31

The close of a year that has been so fruitful – In the course of the year I have advanced my literary reputation, and have been elected an honorary member of the Institute of Paris, and a Fellow of the Royal Society of London. My practice has considerably increased, but my strength and health have more than decreased in proportion.

1833

21 – (*December*)
My family and all my servants etc. take up their abode at 20
Steyne (*Brighton*) – farewell for ever to Castle Place ... So ends
1833: and I begin the world de novo!

1834

*Mantell had set up his collection in the drawing-room of the house in
Brighton:*

May 1
... My reception in this town has certainly been very flattering
so far as visitors and visitings have been concerned but my professional prospects are not encouraging: still I have no right to
complain at present, time and exertion will yet do much for me,
and my noble friend Lord Egremont, whose liberality has placed
me beyond all immediate want of money, having given me a
thousand pounds! still countenances me in the most flattering
manner. All the principal persons in this place have called upon
me, and invited me to their houses; and among many hundreds of
acquaintances I may rank some real friends ... My museum has
been visited by nearly a thousand persons ...

23 (*June*) *Monday*
Rose at four, and at five left Brighton with Mrs Mantell and the
four children, in a carriage and pair for Petworth House; arrived
at Pulborough at ½ past 8 ... and reached the Earl of Egremont's
by twelve. His Lordship received us with great kindness, and
took us over his magnificent residence, and delightful plantations:
we took an early dinner with his Lordship, and after a most
gratifying visit left his Lordship at five ... arrived home at half
past ten. A very delightful excursion.

1835

*At the beginning of this year, Gideon Mantell catalogues his good
fortunes; at the end of it everything seems to have gone wrong –
notably, his home-life was coming to its end as his family was expected
to live in more and more of a museum.*

25 (*December*)
One of the most miserable *Xmas* days I have ever spent.

31st December
The last day of 1835! Went to the Pantomime with the children. What misery have I not endured this year! Several gentlemen met at my house to take into consideration the proposals of myself, Mr Ricardo and H. Smith to offer my Museum for public exhibition.

1836

April 25th
My family removed to Southover and I to lodgings on the Steyne – My collection to be arranged for public exhibition for 2¾ years – but I am sick of the cold-blooded creatures I am surrounded by . . .

Friday – (November)
Received from Messrs Longman 60 copies of the Geol. S.E. of England – and thus close the acct. of the first Edition – when these 60 are sold at 20/- each – I shall clear about £100 by the work – the only money I ever obtained from any literary production.

18 –
. . . Left town at 3 o'clock and reached home (alas! I have no home) soon after 9.

From now on until its end in 1852, Gideon Mantell's journal is a tale of much frustration. He had the fame and honours he desired – but never in the manner he considered fitting. A diary is often spoken of by its writer as a friend; in the case of Gideon Mantell it is clear that more often than not he looked upon his journal as his only friend. As his editor, E. Cecil Curwen decides rather sadly: 'his ambition was not so much to serve mankind as to make himself a name, a form of selfishness which can bring no true satisfaction.'

Marjory Fleming, 1803–1811

Before Marjory Fleming was nine years old, she died of complications following an attack of measles. Between six and a little over eight, she wrote a journal which has found a curious place of its own in literary history. Marjory belonged to a comfortable Scottish family, and was related by way of a lot of cousinship and in-lawdom to Sir Walter Scott. This really was a very distant connection, but Marjory's early editor and biographer made a great thing of it. He was Dr John Brown, author of the once-popular *Rab and his Friends*. Dr Brown sat Marjory firmly on the lap of the great Sir Walter, reciting Shakespeare for his approval. It is from a much later and more scrupulous editing, by Frank Sidgwick, that the extracts here have been chosen.

For three years, Marjory lived with her aunt, Mrs Keith. Her cousin Isabella, or Isa, undertook her education. The journals seem to have been Isabella's idea – partly as an exercise, and partly perhaps as a progress report to be shown eventually to Marjory's parents. The entries have no day-by-day dating, but we know that the work was done between 1809 and 1811; it was in the November of that year that Marjory died, a month or two short of her ninth birthday.

The journals are written in three plain exercise books, together with some verses and a few letters. They retain all the originality of Marjory's own spelling, marked for correction by Isabella. These books, the life work of Marjory Fleming, have the distinction of being housed today in the National Library of Scotland.

G

Many people are hanged for Highway robbery Housebreking
Murder etc. etc. Isabella teaches me everything I know and I am
much indebted to her she is learnen witty & sensible. – I can but
make a poor reward for the servises she has done me if I can give
her any but I doubt it. – repent & be wise saith the preacher before

it be to late. – Regency b nnets are become very fashionable of
late & everybody gets them save poor me but if I had one it
would not become me. – A Mirtal is a beautifull plant & so is
a Geramem and nettel Geramem Climbing is a talent which the
bear excels in and so does monkeys apes & baboons. – I have
been washing my dools cloths today and I like it very much
people who have a good Concience is always happy, but those
who have a bad one is always unhappy and discontented There is
a dog that yels continualy and I pity him to the bottom of my
heart indeed I do. Tales of fashionable life are very good storys
Isabella campels me to sit down & not to rise till this page is done
but it is very near finished only one line to write . . .

*Marjory travels about among her aunts and cousins. The place she
loves above others is Braehead:*

The vision is most beautiful Breahead is a beautiful place & on a
charming situation I should like to see the Exibition very much
& still more so the theater I am reading the misteris of udolpho
with Isabella & am much interested with them I have got some of
Popes works by hart & like them very much. the days are very
long and very light just now which is very pleasant to me and I
darsay to every body. I should like to go and see the curosities in
Londen but I should be a little affraid of the robbers For that
country is greatly infested with them at Edinburgh their is not so
many of them . . .

Today O today I am going to Breahead . . . There the wind
houles to the waves dashing roar but I would not weep my woes
there upon any account . . .

Here I pas my life in rurel filicity festivity & pleasure I

saunter about the woods & forests ... the Trees & hedges are
the most beautiful for they are of the most pretty green I ever
beheld in all my life ...

Here begins Marjory's second Journal:

The Day of my existence here has been delightful & enchantint-
ing. On Saturday I expected no less than three well made Bucks
the names of whom is here advertised Mr. Geo. Crakey and Wm
        <u>are</u>

Keith and Jn Keith, the first is the funniest of every one of them
Mr. Crakey & I walked to Crakeyhall hand by hand in Innocence
and matitation sweet thinking on the kind love which flows in our
    <u>ed</u>

tenderhearted mind which is overflowsing with majestick
pleasure nobody was ever so polite to me in the hole state of my
existence.   <u>w</u>

Mr Craky you must know is a great Buck & pretty good-
looking ... I confess that I have been more like a little young
Devil then a creature for when Isabella went up the stairs to
    <u>a</u>

teach me religion and my multiplication and to be good and all
my other lessons I stamped with my feet and threw my new hat
which she had made me on the ground and was sulky and
was dreadfuly passionate but she never whiped me but gently
                                        <u>p</u>

said Marjory go into another room and think what a great crime
n you are committing ~~and~~ letting your temper git the better of
                                            <u>e</u>

you but I went sulkely that the Devil got the better of me but
    <u>i</u>

she never never whips me so that I thinke I would be the better
of it and the next time that I behave ill I think she should do it
for she never does it but she is very indulgent to me but I am
very ungratefll to hir ...

I am now going to tell you about the horrible and wretched
plaege that my multiplication gives me you cant concieve it — the

most Devilish thing is 8 times 8 & 7 times 7 it is what nature itselfe cant endure

I have a delight^{fu}l pleasure in view which is the thoughts of going to Braehead where I will walk to Craky-hall wich puts me

In mind that I walked to that delightfull place with that delightfull place young man beloved by all his friends and espacialy by me his loveress but I must not talk any longer about hin any longer for Isa said it is not proper for to speak of gentalman but I will never forget him ...

I am going to turn over a new life & am going to be a very good girl & be obedient to Isa Keith, here there is planty of goosberys which makes my teath watter ...

Marjory's third Journal:

Bountifullness and Mercifulness are always rewarded, Isabella has admi_{ra}ble patience in teaching me musick and resignation in perfection In my travels I met with a handsome lad named Charles Balfour Esq, and from him I got ofers of marage ...

The English have great power over the franch; Ah me peradventure, at this moment some noble Colnel at this moment sinks to the ground without breath; — & in convulsive pangs dies; it is a melancoly consideration ... Yesterday a marrade named Mr John Balfour Esq offered to kiss me, & offered to marry me though the man was espused, & his wife was prsent, & said he must ask her permision but he did not I think he was ashamed or confounded before 3 gentelman Mr Jobson & two Mr Kings ...

... Grandure reagns in London & in Edinburgh there are a great many balls & routs but none here. — The childish deses distempers are very frequent just now

... A sailor called here to say farewell, it must be dreadfull to leave his native country where he might get a wife or perhaps me, for I love him ~~very~~ ^{him} very much & wⁱth all my heart, but O I forgot Isabella forbid me to speak about love . . .

There is a book thats is caled the Newgate Calender that contains all the Murders, — all the Murders I say, nay all Thefts & Forgeries that ever _{were} ∧ commited. & fills one with horror & consternation . . .

My address to Isabella on her return, Dear Isabella you are a true lover of nature thou layest down thy head like the meak mountain lamb who draws its last sob by the side of its dam, taken fom hill Villean ^r a poem by Walter Scott & a most beautifull one it is indeed . . .

People who steal & murder bring eternal damnation in the next world upon them, ^{selves} as well as unhappiness in this world. — Adam and Eve dissibayed God. The scarlet fefer is like a plague just now.

Marjory was apparently recovering from measles when she was suddenly taken desperately ill, perhaps with meningitis, and in three days she was dead.

Benjamin Armstrong, 1817–1890

Parsons make good diarists. Their lives may not be packed with sensation but they are certainly packed with people. Perhaps the most famous of all parsonical diarists is James Woodforde, and yet his *Diary of a Country Parson* seems to offer less to the reader than those of two nineteenth-century parsons whose careers overlapped for nine years in spite of the considerable difference in their ages. The first of these, born in 1817 two years after the Battle of Waterloo, is Benjamin Armstrong.

In 1850, when he was thirty-three years old, Armstrong became vicar of East Dereham in Norfolk. He held the living until 1888; this is the period covered by his diary, called *A Norfolk Diary*, and edited by his grandson. Armstrong inclined towards the so-called Oxford Movement, he was rather High Church, and was therefore often in conflict with authority. He writes calmly, with a reserved humour, and we learn very little of his personal affairs. 'My wife', he writes occasionally; 'my younger son'. That is the limit of intimate revelation, yet one seems to know him well. His style of writing, in fact, has much in common with the county in which he lived and worked – flat but peaceful, calm rather than dramatic, but full of subtle delights for any prepared to look for them.

Benjamin Armstrong worked a long, full life. He retired in 1888, and died only two years later.

A Norfolk Diary, 1850–1888

1850

September 14

Having this day been instituted by the Bishop of Norwich to the Vicarage of East Dereham, with the perpetual curacy of Hoe annexed, it becomes my duty to give some account of the place which, with God's blessing, is to be the scene of my future labours ... East Dereham, says the guide-book, is one of the handsomest market towns in Norfolk, 16 miles from Norwich and 100 from London ... The church, dedicated to St Nicholas, is magnificent. It is supported by beautiful clustered pillars, has a tower open to the body of the church, four side-chapels, an antique chest, splendid open seats, a superb font, a brass eagle, and a detached bell-tower containing eight bells. What more need be added but to say that the streets of the town are well paved, named and lighted by gas! There is a good market-house, corn hall, assembly rooms, railway station, excellent schools, some good residences, and a small theatre ... With the exception of one earnest-minded Evangelical and a young Anglo-Catholic priest, I cannot say much for the numerous neighbouring clergy. Indifferentism is the prevailing feeling among them, and the farm, the Petty Sessions, or the Union Board are their occupations. They live like educated and well-disposed country gentlemen, and seem to have no taste for the 'work of the ministry'. The lay people, however, are well disposed towards the Church, which is the more praiseworthy in a period of great religious excitement.

1851

In June I visited London to see the Great Exhibition. It will suffice to mention how overpowering the sight was, and beyond all description grand. The things which pleased me most were the malachite doors from Russia; the furniture, books, and statues from Austria; the stained glass from France; and the exquisite treasures in the Medieval Room. Any attempt to enumerate the chief objects of beauty would be useless. The world never saw such a sight before, and, probably, will never see such a one again.

1852

One day while riding through Longham I perceived the posts and wires of an electric telegraph stretching across the fields from the chief farmer's house to the Parsonage. Fearing that a railway was in contemplation, I enquired of a labouring man a solution of the enigma.

'Sir,' he replied, (with a most knowing look, and indicating the houses with his forefinger) 'there be a young gentleman as lives here, and a young lady as lives there, and they tell me (looking incredulous) that they talk to one another by means of them wires.' What would our forefathers have thought of making love by means of an electric telegraph!

16 *July*

Visited a parishioner of the undoubted age of 102. He claims to be 111, but 102 is his age according to the Parish Register. He is in possession of all his faculties, good-looking, and very neat and careful in his person. Having lived some years in George II's reign, it is no wonder that he has a perfect recollection of the Coronation of George III.

1854

January 1

Drove to take service at Hoe in a sleigh, the snow being too deep for wheels. Had some difficulty in getting through a drift where the horse was above his knees in snow. There were nineteen communicants, and I can hardly tell how they got through the snow to church.

February 16

Active preparations for war. Ten thousand of our troops sail for the East this week. Three magnificent fleets are formed, one for the Channel, one for the Black Sea, and one for the Baltic. They say that the last may be at Yarmouth for a time, in which case one may have an opportunity of seeing it.

March 27

Our fleets are in the Baltic and the Black Sea. The Queen is represented as being much overcome on their leaving, and steamed a little way with them in the *Fairy*.

May 10

A chemist in Dereham showed me a huge box which he filled weekly with pills for a travelling quack, who always disposed of his stock in that time. They were made, he said, of soap and other things which could do no harm.

September 12

. . . a lady told me that the dead in London were being removed in carts as in the time of the Plague, and that policemen were stationed at each end of Silver Street, Regent Street (a healthy portion of town), to prevent anyone entering it, as the cholera is ravaging it. I am told that the following was done at Norwich, where the pestilence is also very bad: a piece of fresh meat being attached to a kite was flown into the air for a couple of hours. When the kite descended, the meat was black and putrid. This would make it seem that the cause of cholera is in the air rather than arising from noxious vapours from the earth. It is also said that there is something so deadly in the atmosphere that in Paris innumerable swallows fall down dead, and that these summer visitants, notwithstanding the heat of the weather, have taken their departure from many parts of England much sooner than usual.

November 20

A good day at cottage work, and a most numerous attendance at Evensong. On the fifth of this month a most terrific combat ensued between the English and the Russians at Balaclava. The enemy lost 8000 men and the English 2500. No less than 102 of our officers and 3 generals – Lords Cathcart, Goldie and Strangeways – were slain, and 5 more generals were wounded. We claim the victory, but it can scarce be called one at so dear a purchase. Sebastapol still holds out. Grief and enthusiasm are at their height. A disaster was caused by an error on the part of Captain Nolan.

He was sent with a message from Lord Raglan to the cavalry, to the effect that they were to charge if practicable. He forgot to add this condition, and hence the slaughter of the poor fellows who bravely rushed to certain destruction. Nolan himself was slain, and the Duke of Cambridge had his horse killed under him. May these heroes rest in peace!

November 26
In the afternoon the congregation was large, and the large chandelier and pulpit candles being lighted gave an air of great comfort and warmth to our very cold church. Preached on the discipline of the body and drew a strong picture of the praise-worthy efforts of the female poor in clothing their families – the great need of clothing where so many 'gangs' of women and children work in the fields. It is astonishing how the poor contrive to live. Although the end of November I gathered a pretty bouquet in my garden stroll which I always take between services – China roses, double stocks, salvias, mignonette etc., which seem bloom-ing 'out of due time'.

December 19
The 400 loaves given annually on St Thomas's Day usually cause such confusion in the church, and in the hurry so many get them who ought not, that I determined this year to select the most deserving persons. I drove over the whole parish for this purpose.

December 21 *St Thomas*
The gifts as usual brought a large number to church, and many who had come only for the sake of them were much disgusted when told that they had previously been given to the poorest and most deserving.

1855

January 31
Our army in the Crimea is decimated and suffering unheard-of privations. In the Parliamentary debates it appears that the whole affair has been most shamefully mismanaged, and that, to use the words of Mr B. Osborne, 'the condition of the British Army is

rotten to the core'. Our Allies carry our sick, lend us 2000 greatcoats, and in short do our work for us . . .

February 24
Intense cold, tens of thousands out of employment, bread riots have taken place in Liverpool and London. Our army is destroyed. The Cabinet is continually changing. And yet we see no greater or more devout attendance on the ordinances of religion, or any signs of a nation's belief in God's Providence, beyond a chat in the House of Lords about a 'Day of humiliation.'

April 25
The Emperor and Empress of the French have returned to Paris after their week's visit to the Queen. It is said that all things are ready for them to go to Sebastapol to superintend the siege personally.

May 23
Worked hard all the morning among the sick and distressed in order to have time for a little trout-fishing in the evening . . .

1856

March 30 Sunday
While I was preaching in the morning on the text *Peace be unto you* the Tower guns must have been proclaiming the welcome news that the treaty was signed in Paris whereby the war is happily terminated, and peace ensured to the nations. At Evensong we used the Thanksgiving for Peace, and I set the bells going immediately.

For some years the diary is concerned with parish matters, about warming the church – or partly warming it; about charity funds and garden parties, where croquet has been 'quite superceded' by lawn tennis. And about doctrine and local government, in which there seems a good deal of ill-feeling between the farmers and the rest of society. There are school feasts, sermons preached in neighbouring parishes, family visits to the seaside. On 29th January 1861 it is briefly noted that 'The Southern American States have revolted against the

Northern, and a fierce Civil War is said to be imminent.' *Then we are into the '70s and there is the Franco-Prussian war and the Zulu war to add drama to everyday life. As Benjamin Armstrong observes these from his Norfolk parish, Francis Kilvert's diary is just beginning to be written . . .*

Francis Kilvert, 1840–1879

The second of the two nineteenth century parson-diarists is Francis Kilvert, who was born on the other side of England, in Wiltshire, when Benjamin Armstrong was already twenty-three years old. His diary starts in 1870, when he had been for some little time curate at Clyro in Radnorshire, after a spell as his father's curate. In the course of the diary, Kilvert returns to his father for a time, then in 1887 he becomes vicar of Bredwardine in Herefordshire. Although he is constantly falling in love with girls who seem to him as beautiful as a dream, Kilvert remains single to the end of the diary. In fact, he married in that same year, 1879. He was thirty-nine. The wedding was in August and not quite a month later he died of peritonitis.

Like Armstrong, Kilvert seems to reflect the character of the country in which he worked. The dramatic beauty of the countryside in and about the Welsh border is admirably suited to such an emotional, enthusiastic, easily-despairing nature. What is more, his parishioners seem to laugh or weep just as readily and as easily as he does. Kilvert is really a poet, but his feelings too often run away with him. He seems to pour everything into his diary, so that at times the reader is bound to feel an eavesdropper. For all that, he is aware, and says as much, that the journal may one day be read by strangers.

Kilvert's Diary, 1870–1879

Francis Kilvert had been curate at Clyro in Radnorshire for five years when he commenced his diary in 1870. It is a very copious and fluent affair in three volumes, but even those three are the result of editing twenty-two tightly filled notebooks. William Plomer, who edited the work, has also made a shortened version in one volume, which retains all the savour of the longer publication.

1870

Wednesday 16 March

I ate so much hare that I could hardly walk and saw stars, but at 4 went up the hill by the Bron, Penllan and Little Wern y Pentre ... passing by the Great Twyns which I am happy to see is falling into ruin, the window frames falling in. How well I remember and how short a time ago it seems though nearly five years. I never pass the house without thinking of that afternoon when after neglecting Margaret Thomas's dying son for a long time I went to call and was inexpressibly shocked to find that he had died only ten minutes before.

5th April

... We crossed a field and the fold of a farm house, scrambled down a narrow stony lane and struck the main road again. About a mile above Llanthony we descried the Abbey ruins, the dim grey pile of building in the vale below standing by the little river side among its brilliant green meadows. What was our horror on entering the enclosure to see two tourists with staves and shoulder belts all complete postured among the ruins in an attitude of admiration, one of them of course discoursing learnedly to his gaping companion and pointing out objects of interest with his stick. If there is one thing more hateful than another it is being told what to admire and having objects pointed out to one with a stick. Of all noxious animals too the most noxious is a tourist. And of all tourists the most vulgar, illbred, offensive and loathsome is the British tourist ...

Thursday, 7 April
I had the satisfaction of managing to walk from Hay to Clyro by the fields without meeting a single person, always a great triumph to me and a subject for warm self congratulation for I have a peculiar dislike to meeting people, and a peculiar liking for a deserted road.

Saturday, 16 July
To-day we heard rumours of war and war itself. Henry Dew brought the news stated in the *Globe* that war had been declared by France against Prussia, the wickedest, most unjust most unreasonable war that ever was entered into to gratify the ambition of one man. I side with the Prussians and devoutly hope the French may never push France to the Rhine.

Tuesday, 20 September
From the stile on the top of the hill above the plantation watched the sun set in a crimson ball behind the hills or rather into a dense ball of dark blue vapour. It was like seeing a sunset over the sea. He went down very fast. All the country round was full of evening sounds, children's voices, dogs barking, the clangour of geese. Meanwhile the sheep fed quietly round me. Then came the afterglow round the S. and E. Scarlet feathers floated in the sky, and the gorse deepened into a rich redder gold in the sunset light.

Saturday, 29 October
... Last night we heard that Metz has fallen and that four Marshals of France and 150,000 men have surrendered as prisoners of war ... Today I found in a book a red silk handkerchief worked with the words 'Forget me not', and I am sorry to say that I have entirely forgotten who gave it to me ...

Wednesday, 16 November
Last night the waning moon shone bright and cold in the East and I had a horrible dream that I was married to Mrs Danzey and living as curate at Gwythian. I woke up in a cold sweat ...

Wednesday, 28 December (in Wiltshire, his home)
An inch of snow fell last night and as we walked to Draycot to skate the snow storm began again. As we passed Langley Burrell Church we heard the strains of the quadrille band on the ice at Draycot. The afternoon grew murky and when we began to skate the air was thick with falling snow. But it soon stopped and gangs of labourers were at work immediately sweeping away the new fallen snow and skate cuttings of ice. The Lancers was beautifully skated. When it grew dark the ice was lighted with Chinese lanterns, and the intense glare of blue, green and crimson lights and magnesium riband made the whole place as light as day. Then people skated with torches.

1871

Friday 3 February
This evening we had our 4th Penny Reading. The room was fuller than ever, crammed, people almost standing on each other's heads, some sitting up on the high window-seats ... Numbers could not get into the room and hung and clustered round the windows outside ... The heat was fearful and the foul air gave me a crushing headache and almost stupefied me. I recited Jean Ingelow's 'Reflections' and my own 'Fairy Ride'.

March Day (i.e. 1st March; 2nd is March Morrow; the last day of February is March Eve. And so throughout the year.)
After dinner last night Mr V. kindly anxious to cure my face ache made me drink four large glasses of port. The consequence was that all today I have been groaning with a bursting raging splitting sick headache.

April Eve
A letter ... asking me to go to Whitney Rectory ... to meet Miss Hutchinson, the niece of William Wordsworth by marriage and the god-daughter of his sister Dorothy, for whom I have a great admiration.

Friday, 8 September
Perhaps this may be a memorable day in my life ... Today I fell in love with Fanny Thomas.

'Fanny' Thomas's real name was Daisy. Poor Kilvert gets into a great state about her. 'I have been in a fever all day about Daisy, restless and miserable with uncertainty.' 'A wretched, restless, feverish night.' *When Kilvert asks Daisy's father if he may hope for her hand, Mr Thomas is very put out, or* 'seemed a good deal taken aback', *as Kilvert says. Perhaps the young curate is not very surprised about that, for he admits himself:* 'On this day when I proposed for the girl who will I trust one day be my wife I had only one sovereign in the world, and I owed that.' *In spite of all the groaning and fever, Francis Kilvert did not marry his Daisy – indeed he is fairly soon in love with someone else, and consulting the sympathetic Mrs Venables, the vicar's wife* 'about my love affairs'. *Fortunately there comes a distraction – the Prince of Wales is desperately ill and is expected to die.*

Thursday, 14 *December*
The anniversary of the Prince Consort's death ten years ago, and people were very anxious about it for it was said the Prince of Wales was conscious of the day, but to-day the Prince is better. Thank God.

Sunday, 17 *December*
Before he began his sermon this morning Mr Venables read from the pulpit the latest telegram from Sandringham which is very comfortable. 'The prince has passed a tranquil day and the symptoms continue to be favourable.' Dated last evening. What a blessed happy contrast to the suspense and fear of last Sunday. How thankful we all are. I love that man now, and always will love him. I will never say a word against him again. God bless him. God bless him and keep him, the Child of England. In the afternoon I alluded to the Prince's illness in an old Advent sermon on John the Baptist from Matthew XI, 10 and nearly broke down.

Wednesday, 27 *December*
... At the cross roads we met Mrs Ashe with Thersie and Syddy going round to the cottages giving the invitations to the New Year's supper at Langley House. Syddy is magnificent entirely,

splendidly handsome. I never thought her so beautiful before. Her violet eyes, her scarlet lips, the luxuriance of her rich chestnut curling hair, indescribable . . .

1872

Tuesday, 16 January
. . . Called on Lewis the policeman who was in a difficulty to know what to do with some Clyro boys who had been playing football on Sunday.

Saturday, 20 January
Took old Sylvanus Whitcome a note from the Registers showing that he was baptised January 1st 1783 . . .

Tuesday, 23 January
Visited Edward Evans, old Price the paralysed keeper, Mrs Lacy, Catherine Ferris, James Smith and Mrs Price of the Swan who showed me preserved in a box part of one of Price's whiskers pulled out by the Clyro women in the late row at the Swan . . .

Wednesday, 24 January
Visited John Morgan. The old soldier had another epileptic fit on Sunday . . .

Saturday, 13 April
The two old women Hannah Jones and Sarah Probert were both lying in bed and groaning horribly. I gave them some money and their cries and groans suddenly ceased.

June Eve
. . . Today is Minna Venables' birthday . . . Flags were flying over Clyro School and children were swarming in and out like bees. Over the school gate the schoolmaster and mistress had made a pretty triumphal arch of greenery and flowers with 'Long Live Miss Venables'. As we dashed up to the Vicarage door the bells pealed out. They had been ringing since early morning and the ringers had dined at the Vicarage. The blacksmiths also had been firing anvil cannons since 5.30 a.m. The children had their tea on

the lawn between 5 and 6 o'clock ... It seemed as if the night would never get dark and we could not begin the fireworks till nearly ten. They were the first fireworks ever seen in Clyro ...

This year young Kilvert gives up his curacy and applies to the Bishop for preferment. The Bishop is unresponsive. Kilvert returns to Langley Burrell to be his father's curate once more. The people of Clyro are distressed.

Tuesday, 4 June
The news of my leaving Clyro is spreading through the village. These people will break my heart with their affectionate lamentation.

Saturday, 22 June
... I found on my table a red leather case containing a beautiful gold watch and chain with two most kind letters from Mr and Mrs Venables ...

Thursday, 27 June
Mrs Baskerville sent a kind letter ... saying that she and her daughters wished me to carry away some remembrance of them and begging me to take my choice of an oaken stationery cabinet, a large musical box, a time piece or a fitted travelling bag ...

Friday, 28 June
... Going down the village I fell in with old James Jones the sawyer. 'I hear you are going away,' he said in a broken trembling voice. And he walked down the village with me weeping as he went.

Tuesday, 9 July
... the children deputed little Amy Evans (of whom they know I am very fond) to present to me a little box in which I found a beautiful gold pencil case to hang on my watch chain. My own precious lambs ... I tried to speak to tell them what I felt, but my heart was full.

Friday, 12 July
Daisy gave me a rose.

Showered with gifts, with tears and lamentations, Francis Kilvert comes to his last day at Clyro:

Sunday, 25 August
I read prayers in the morning. Irvine preached and Mr Venables sat in his pew. Irvine and I walked to Bettws. It was my last visit to the dear old Chapel. Every tree and hill and hollow and glimpse of the mountains was precious to me, and I was walking with a stranger to whom it was naught, and who had no dear associations with the place. I took the whole service and preached a farewell sermon from Philippians 1, 3. 'I thank my God upon every remembrance of you.' It was for the last time. I could not help it. I burst into tears. After chapel I went to Chapel Farm and Llyn Gwillim and to the Forge and sweet Emma of the Chapel Dingle to say Goodbye and then to Whitty's Mill, the dear old Mill, to see sweet dying Margaret. It was a sad sad day.

The last five years of the diary include a brief return to Clyro and a, last encounter with Daisy. On Tuesday the 3rd November 1874 Francis Kilvert wrote:

'Why do I keep this voluminous journal? I can hardly tell. Partly because life appears to me such a curious and wonderful thing that it almost seems a pity that even such a humble and uneventful life as mine should pass altogether away without some such record as this and partly too because I think the record may amuse and interest some who come after me.'

Augustus Hare, 1834–1903

Augustus Hare, a vain and trivial man, filled six whole volumes with an account of a vain and trivial life. He was a copious letter-writer, and frequently sent chunks of his journal as a means of communicating with his friends – so one can imagine him carefully taking copies for posterity, which was certainly intended to learn about him.

Augustus's diary is packed with social information, and gives a sharp and convincing picture of life in what used to be called 'high society' in late Victorian and Edwardian days. The changes in manners are noted and deplored, as they always will be by the outgoing generation. Augustus Hare was well connected and had the entrée into big houses up and down England, where he was almost sure to find a cousin, or a cousin's cousin. He delighted in it all. As he travels to stay with the Duke or the Earl, as he flatters Lord Y. and Lady X., one has a vision of him planning his year around the establishments of the wealthy, and making sure that his invitations fit with one another to ensure the maximum usefulness. This kept him busy, and with that and his diary and the many books of travel he wrote to keep him in funds, he was at least not idle. He lived solitary after the death of his stepmother, to whom he was extravagantly devoted. Augustus is mentioned in Francis Kilvert's diary, for in his youth he had been one of many pupils tutored by Kilvert's father.

Kilvert's entry for the 15th November 1870 mentions a letter from Augustus Hare, which tells him of Mrs Hare's fatal illness and recalls the old days at the Rectory. 'It all seems very long ago,' Augustus writes, 'but so vivid still, the garden with its laurel hedges and the large elm tree, the dusty hot little courtyard, the romantic adventures of climbing down by stealth into the vault under the church, persuading Mary the cook to give us hot little cakes of bread out of the window when she was cooking ...' Next day, Kilvert learns of Mrs Hare's death. 'Poor Augustus, what will he do without her? She has been his object in life.'

His object in life thereafter became himself. He is possibly the biggest '*I*' among all these diarists. Still, he undoubtedly has some style, and he is an invaluable authority for anyone studying his period.

The Story of My Life

1878

November 29th (at Burghley House, Stamford)
I have been glad to come to the place which is often called 'the finest House in England' – a dictum in which I by no means agree. The guests are a row of elderly baronets of only hunting and Midland-county fame. I took a Miss Fowke in to dinner, and complained to her of the number of old baronets. 'Yes,' she said, 'they are old and they are numerous, and the central one is my father.'

The house is immense, but has little internal beauty. There is a series of stately rooms, dull and oppressive, with fine tapestry and china, and a multitude of pictures with very fine names, almost all misnamed.

Lord Exeter, with his lank black hair and his wrinkled yellow jack-boots high above the knee, looks like a soldier of Cromwell. In the evening, he and the whole family dance incessantly to the music of a barrel-organ, which they take it in turn to wind.

1879

May 19th
The Prince (*of Sweden and Norway – Augustus was very friendly with this particular Royal family*) has arrived with his suite at Claridge's. He received me most cordially and affectionately.

We made many plans for sight-seeing and people-seeing, but in England I have no responsibility . . .

I dined at charming Lady Wynford's, sitting near Lord Delamere, who was very full of a definition he had heard of the word 'deputation'. 'A noun of multitude, which signifies many, but not much.' It was attributed to Gladstone, who said, 'I only wish I *had* made it.' Lord Eustace Cecil produced a definition of 'Independent Member' as 'a Member on whom nobody can depend.'

There was an immense gathering at Lady Salisbury's afterwards, my Prince there and much liked. There, for the first time, I saw the Empress Augusta of Germany.

May 29th
At dinner at Lord Carysfort's and ball at Lady Salisbury's, I presented so many relations to the Prince that he said what astonished him more than anything else in England was 'the multitude of Mr Hare's cousins.'

1882

October 7th
Yesterday we went by appointment to Welbeck, arriving by the darksome tunnel, more than two miles long, upon which the late Duke (*he was the fifth Duke of Portland*) spent £60,000, and £60,000 more apiece upon banking up (and spoiling) his sheet of water with brick walls and building a gigantic riding-school. The house itself stands well, considering the ugliness of the park, and is rather handsome . . .

The late Duke lived almost entirely in a small suite of rooms in the old part of the house. He inherited the peculiarity of his mother, who would see no one, and he always hid himself . . . When he went to London it was in a closed brougham, which was put on a railway truck, and which deposited him at his own house in Cavendish Square, his servants all being ordered out of the way: no one ever saw him go or arrive. When he needed a doctor, the doctor only came to the door, and asked questions through it of the valet, who was allowed to feel his pulse.

The Duke's mania for a hidden life made him build immense

suites of rooms underground, only approachable by a common
flight of steps leading to a long tunnel, down which the dinner is
conveyed from the far-distant kitchen on a tramway. From a
great library one enters a billiard-room capable of holding half-a-
dozen billiard-tables. A third large room leads to an enormous
ball-room, which can contain 2000 people. The approach to this
from above is by means of a gigantic hydraulic drop, in which a
carriage can be placed, or twenty persons can be accommodated –
the guests being thus let down to the ball-room itself. A staircase
through the ceiling of one of the rooms, which is drawn up by a
windlass, leads hence to the old riding-school, which is lighted by
1000 jets of gas. Hence a tunnel, 200 yards long, leads to a
quadrangle piece of ground, unbuilt on, but excavated in pre-
paration for a large range of bachelors rooms, smoking rooms,
and nurseries, to cover four acres of ground. Another tunnel,
three-quarters of a mile long, leads thence to the stables, cow-
houses, and dairies, like a large village ... At the Duke's death
there were ninety-four horses in the stables, only trained for
exercise or feeding. Beyond the stables is a large riding-school
in which there are 8000 jets of gas, and exercising ground under
glass, with a gallop on straw and sawdust for a quarter of a mile.
Close by is an enormous garden, of which six acres are used for
strawberry beds, every alternate row being glazed for forcing the
plants ... The garden is about thirty acres in extent and requires
fifty-three men. In the late Duke's time there were forty-five
grooms and helpers in the stables ... There were eight keepers
and underkeepers.

All is vast, splendid and utterly comfortless; one could imagine
no more awful and ghastly fate than waking up one day and
finding oneself Duke of Portland and master of Welbeck!

1887

September 7th

I came here through the lovely Church Stretton country, stopping
at picturesque Shrewsbury on the way to stay with the Bishop of
Lichfield and Augusta.

Augusta had many interesting reminiscences of Lord Beacons-
field. One day, at luncheon, she offered him the mustard. 'I never

take mustard,' he replied in his sepulchral voice. 'Oh, don't
you?' she said airily. 'No,' he continued in solemnest tones. 'There
are three things I have never used: I have never touched mustard;
I have never had a watch; and I have never made use of an
umbrella.' — 'Well,' said Augusta, 'I can understand the mustard
— that is a mere matter of taste; but surely going without the other
things must have been sometimes rather inconvenient.' — 'And
why should I want them?' continued Disraeli more sepulchrally
than ever. 'I live under the shadow of Big Ben, and there is a
clock in every room of the House of Commons, so that I cannot
possibly require a watch; and as I always go about in a close
carriage, I can never want an umbrella.' Disraeli was always full of
these small affectations.

1892

The summer of 1892 was full of quiet pleasures. Visits leave little
to be remembered except the pleasant parties and the extreme
kindness of hosts and hostesses everywhere. I am indeed glad
my visiting-lines are cast in such pleasant places, that I so seldom
have to consort with the drearier part of human nature. In these
houses, where the conversation is perfectly charming, yet where
no evil is spoken of any one or by any one, one sees truly how a
christian spirit will christianise everything it touches.

Ivy Jacquier

The Jacquier family of four girls and two boys had a French Catholic
father and an English Protestant mother. The children naturally enough
grew up bi-lingual, and probably bi-partizan in both a patriotic and religious
sense. Ivy passionately loved France, where the family home was, but she
eventually married an Englishman and settled in Worcestershire. Her
published diaries begin with her schooldays and end in 1926, the final entry
speaking of a Christmas party for her daughter, Sally. The extracts here are
taken from the first year of the diary, when Ivy, aged sixteen, was at boarding-
school in Eastbourne, enduring all the glooms and exaltations of adolescence.
She writes often with pomposity, and in a rather high-flown style which
remains in the later diaries. But there is plenty of humour, too, and she
frequently forgets to be anything but a schoolgirl. We find her involved in a
hating relationship with one of the staff, Miss Annie, and a loving friendship
with Gladys – who later married Ivy's brother Léon. She reads enormously
and comments with sternness, and it is easy to see the artistic eye and impulse which later made her a painter. Hers is the second diary of a young girl
to be included in this collection. Marjory Fleming, writing her journal
almost a hundred years earlier, was seven years younger than Ivy, and seven
years covers a lot of childhood. All the same, it is not too impossible to detect
a certain personal quality shared by the two girls – nine-year-old Marjory's
self-analysis is often every bit as strict as Ivy's – though Ivy's is better spelt.

The Diary of Ivy Jacquier, 1907–1926

1907

Jan 22

Wallace Collection with Léon. (*Her brother is in London learning Banking.*) Watteau, Lancret, Pater are *splendid*. Van Dyck's portraits. Go down at 3.22 with school from Victoria. In bed now ... so cold ... and miserable ... so far away! So lonely for sister Doris. Am getting a cold. Feel buzzy and egotistical with a continual big I looming in my thoughts. People forget the horrors of school to remember only the sunny days. That is why they do not truly pity you as you would be pitied. A letter from Doris.

Feb 5

Measles break out! One girl is going home. Lucky beast. The smell of lilies of the valley in my room is lovely. I am glad to go to bed for the pleasure of smelling them. My orange mingles its scent with that of the lilies. I read *Pippa Passes*. It is tragic.

For half an hour today we had a lecture on the Spirit of the Athenians, showing the influence of climate upon temperament and the love of beauty carried to excess. I will never forget this half-hour.

Feb 10

Writing my Diary is now my only comfort. I feel anxious, tormented, unsettled. Bed!

Feb 22

... Miss A. is so ugly. (*She was the headmistress's sister.*) Surely it is needless. Maeterlinck says so. She might prevent some of her hideosity. I have no natural kindness to help me overcome such antipathies. I *hate* her because she is so awful to sit near, awful to look at, awful to hear speak. She likes anemones; it is characteristic of her. She is very kind to me, and she likes me. Oh dear, I wish I was on the sea crossing to Calais today.

Mar 16

Great row with Miss Annie. I hate that woman as I have hated few. She makes me sick. My vaccination has taken well. I would like to live under tree roots today and feel leaves on me. This is the result of Rackham's illustrations. Violet (*another sister*) comes down for my confirmation. I am happy. Miss Annie said she should think I would not be proud to claim France as my country.

Mar 19

Miss Annie made peace this morning. It would have been better not for my morals. How I am expected to knuckle under to someone who abjectly apologises when I am in the wrong is beyond my ken. At 19 I shall be unholdable – a Nero!

Mar 21

I was confirmed with Gladys. I cried and couldn't stop myself.

Mar 22

Miss Annie is dreadful. May I not poison her? . . .

Mar 23

When I am older I shall read a lot of Swinburne. Went to church with Gladys in the evening. The music was good and the Nunc Dimittis well sung. I hate Miss Annie very much even though the sun is so bright and I leave Wednesday. Gladys gives me *The Oxford Book of English Verse* bound in white vellum. I am so happy and excited. I shall love my book more and more and show it to Violet in the train and take great care of it. To think that tomorrow I shall be clasped to the bosom of my family! Oh! to think of it. I am really happy. I am happy now this minute.

At home for the holidays, Ivy Jacquier plays tennis and dances with handsome Tony Wilding – 'Tony waltzes beautifully'; 'Wilding is marvellous and a pleasure to look at' and 'E. sent me a photo of Wilding cut out of newspaper'. *She reads Shelley and George Meredith, but does not mind admitting that she also reads 'Chum's Monthly'. Then it is back to school* –

May 8
I find a flower in my long white coat that I picked during a tennis match. I am sad with the crumpled leaf. Read Marie Corelli coming through the pouring landscape. Unpacked. Am tired. It always seems to be an insult, to be sent to school.

May 17
Disgraceful new rule! We are to confess every Sunday the rules we have broken during the week. I have never been particularly truthful and now shall become a liar.

May 23
Quarrelled with Gladys and made it up again. My tennis is improving, I have been made captain . . .

May 24
Miss Annie makes us fetch and carry for her, Old carrot face! . . .

Old Carrot Face

May 30
Bored with girl species. Come to conclusion school tends to degeneration. It not only kills the germs of natural originality, but encourages pettiness, meanness. It kills kindness and levels one to the prosaic and vulgar. It has no place in its routine for analysis, reflexion. The education stuffs you with detail and

neglects to give you perspective. It utterly neglects the forming of your character. The *one* good derived is a little experience and a spirit of disillusion fitting one for life after ...

June 9

Went out with Miss A. who is a bore. She is too uncritically enthusiastic for a woman of her years. Besides, she is unwieldy, and eats cream on her chocolate blancmange.

July 13

... These days are dull. In a fortnight school will be over. I am just longing to get to the books I have set aside for the holidays.

Aug 3 *(on holiday in Harrogate)*

Gladys writes me she is leaving school. The news makes a landmark in these years. Few big things or sad things have happened to me, and none I ever loved have died. Mother was very ill once, but otherwise joy succeeded joy. Gladys has broken my luck, but even so I shall have enough to share with her if she needs it. Read *Vittoria*, but cannot, all day, forget Gladys's news. At first I wanted never to write to her again ...

Aug 9

Ripping hard game of tennis. Mr D. says I should play well. I'd try like the dickens if that were true; my obstacles are – erratic play, bad sight, unsteady nerve. Waltz with Mr D. He is superb ...

Aug 14

If my technique is ever capable, I shall remember to draw the lines of a tall and beautiful billiard-player such as Mr D. ...

Oct 4

Awful pudding. Dull day. I would have given three days of my life this morning to have slept for another two hours. I have said goodbye to Doris who goes back to France, and now school seems to have begun in all grimness ...

Oct 13
Mother leaves. I do not feel lonely yet as I have Owen Wister's
Virginian to dream of – grey eyed and strong beautiful youth!
Then comes dull long work and my head aches, and we read
Ruskin, and I do not listen and I think Ruskin is a fool.

In this last term at school, Ivy hates Miss Annie more than ever,
misses Gladys, worries about the future – she is to go to Dresden to the
university – philosophises and romanticises:

I would like to go to a fancy dress ball as Clothilde. I see her in
white, with a red rose and great soft thick Roman satin sash,
swimming forward like a Du Maurier drawing, her hair tight
back leaving her eyes bold, and over her shoulders a long sable
stole.

At the last it is suddenly difficult to say goodbye:

Dec 10
Lovely day and ride along the roads on Paddy. Last elocution
lesson with the man-of-the-world, well-shirted Mr Pertwee.
Second wrench; who guessed I should have to tear my habits up in
such painful manner? Third wrench; goodbye to the studio;
goodbye to the bohemian liberty of those evenings, and the walk
back through the lighted town eating an apple as soon as I got
beyond the streets; the frosty air; the cab ranks along the sea front.

Dec 20
Gladys has come for three days. She is not looking very well . . .

Dec 21
Gladys says she is depressed. Perhaps, as I am, by the instability
of human affections . . .

Then she is home:

Dec 30
Doris and I sit in big armchairs by the dining-room fire. We
make toast, then we spread it with dripping . . . In the evening I

have my first, first cigarette. Three slow artistic puffs – I am
born to it!

Dec 31
Goodbye my first diary, dear. The year has brought a few
changes, *all* recorded in these pages.

Medicine and Duty

A WAR DIARY by HAROLD DEARDEN

In his preface to the book, the author apologises for the fact that his diary contains 'an insistence' on his own thoughts and actions, describing it thus: '. . . as a history of the campaign of that period it is lamentably deficient. It is, to a history of the war, what a pantry-book is to the history of a great house.'

The history of a great house, however, is incomplete without such household detail, and so the history of the First World War would be a poor thing without the personal accounts of those who fought in it. The author in this case, comfortably settled in the medical profession, became without hesitation what he chooses to call 'a mere camp-follower'. He was himself wounded while caring for the wounded, and was finally invalided out of the army and returned to civilian life. Although while he was on active service he never doubted what he had to do, and though he was often strangely tranquil about it all, he admits in his preface to moral confusion. 'To succour the wounded, that they might with greater celerity return to wound or be wounded on a subsequent occasion, seemed subtly reminiscent of those dreadful ministrations offered to horses at a bull-fight. For there, too, in drab little places within earshot of the cheering, skilful hands patched and prodded agonised creatures back into the arena. And if in my case the patching was better, the prodding more subtle, and the creature itself even willing to return, these facts merely shifted the plane of the whole grim business from the illogical to the insane . . .'

The diary begins when the author gets to France and ends just before the Armistice; but there is no other dating.

I arrived here a few days ago after a perfectly monstrous crossing, and found my quarters somewhat of a change from one's pre-war consulting rooms. The mess was formerly a cheap restaurant. Not a carpet on the floor anywhere, damp running off the walls, and paper in the rooms which — where it is not begging with the look of one crucified to be put out of its misery and torn from its last slender hold on the wall — is of a colour such as to appall the eye of the beholder ... We have three small lamps in the room, which is about as large as a ten-acre field; and we have fifteen men in the mess. The result is that all three lamps are huddled round the central stove for warmth, and round these four faintly glowing points are clustered all fifteen of the mess ... On the whole it is quieter in one's bedroom than anywhere; but writing with the block on the window-sill is of a coldness outside my previous experience, so I brave the mess instead. I was delighted to-day at lunch to hear a man telling another what a lot of good this war had done to his brother. 'He was a namby pamby sort of chap before, used to read a lot and that sort of thing, you know; no real harm in him but a useless sort of beggar. Now he's had three years as a private in the 3rd London, and he's as decent a fellow as you could want to know!' It is good to know that the war is uplifting people after all, as the Bishop of London so encouragingly said.

I was orderly officer last night, which entails receiving all convoys of wounded, and, incidentally, getting about one hour's sleep; but it's full of interest and human nature. Once when I was standing on the top of the steps about 2.30 a.m., waiting to receive a convoy, a bus full of walking cases unloaded at the gates. As they came along the road up to the door they made a wonderful picture — such typical fighting men, mud-stained and practical, with their steel helmets swung behind them and their bandaged hands and heads and mud-splashed faces and hair. But as the first man came into the full glare of the arcs over the door, it was as though something magical had happened. It took my breath away. Quite gone was the grim khaki figure of a second before, and there, under the faded fancy dress, was just a dog-tired little

cockney, thin neck, adenoids and all. As he saw me standing in
the shadow he gave his pack a pathetic little hitch, pulled himself
up, and saluted with his one good hand – but it was the real heart
of the man that I had seen for that one second when he thought he
was alone . . . I never go to bed here without a look of amazement
over my troubled mind . . .

A little fox terrier has come creeping into the hospital and
taken refuge on the bed of one of the patients who is sleeping
out in the garden. She is a wretched little cowed thing, and
seems half wild with terror, is a mass of dirt and looks as if she has
been chased for miles and stoned. The man is quite pleased to have
her on his bed, and I have told an orderly to get her a plate of
food . . .

The little dog is still great friends with the man she chose first
and lies on his bed all day and night. He has tied a bow of cyanide
gauze round her neck and confided to me today that he has
called her 'Alice' after a dog that he has at home, and that even
already she understands everything he says. As she is a French
dog I should doubt it; but she certainly loves him all right, and
lies up against the cradle over his broken leg as happy as can
be . . .

. . . Went up to the tennis court in the afternoon and watched
the tennis, talked for about three hours to the girls there – to
improve my French! – and was fetched back at six o'clock by an
orderly to see a case who was bleeding. Came back to find a lad
who has a badly shattered knee bleeding pretty badly, and tied
two small vessels. He is only about twenty and a very decent lad.
It seems awful to think sometimes of the number of armless and
legless men we have turned out of this hospital alone. England
will be a quaint place after this is all over.

Another very busy day. A good many cases came in this
morning, several pretty bad. Amputated one boy's leg; he's only
just eighteen, and looks so bad that I doubt if he will live the
night through . . . He's quite conscious now and feeling no pain;
and he just holds your hand and rocks his head from side to side,
and keeps saying, 'I'm all right now, sir; just give me something
to do, anything you like, sir, I'm all right now, sir,' and so on and
on without a pause . . .

The diarist leaves his base hospital, with its tennis and occasional snatched trips to the coast, and moves forward:

. . . It is a perfectly terrible sight to cross this ground newly won from the Germans, with men lying just where they fell, and others in little groups of isolated men, where shell or bullet hit them. One man I saw today . . . had evidently been rushing a trench, and got a bullet through the stomach about twenty yards from his objective. He had thrown away his rifle at once and crawled to a shell hole for cover, and here I found him. He had undone his trousers and pulled up his shirt to see the wound, and died as he looked at it; for he lay there, his two hands holding his dirty shirt up to show a clean red hole in his muddy skin and, with his head fallen forward on his chest, he seemed even now to be wondering what to do next!

. . . The Boche was shelling the village very heavily with 5.9s as we approached, looking for a gun just to the left of it, and there was some anxiety as to his switching off suddenly on to the village itself. The shell-bursts here are really pretty. The earth is a lovely brown, and huge spouts of bright brown earth showing in the evening sun through the trees make a wonderful show. The noise was pretty considerable, however, and great trees were going up like matches, so we were all very glad to get down below. I have got a very good spot, quite dry and recently concreted over, so one ought to get no rats in it. Most charming of all is a swallow's nest in the roof corner, for I can lie and watch the two little creatures bringing in food-stuff and going through all their domestic routine with that happy earnestness which distinguishes birds. It's wonderful how little they mind the noise; and only sometimes, when something big drops really near and jars you like a slap in the face, do they leave the nest and flutter twittering round.

Last night was worse than the night before – at least as far as I was concerned. The road up which the transport comes at night passes just behind my aid post, and as the artillery had been using it during the day to bring up ammunition etc., the Boche opened a barrage of 5.9s on it at ten at night. At 10.45 our transport arrived in the yard behind my aid post, and I went out to see a man who was hit by a splinter. The place was literally all over bits of shrapnel, and I have never seen limbers unloaded in such record time! I was holding my water-bottle in my hand as I came round the corner, and a piece of shrapnel came past like a bullet and went clean through the strap, cutting it in half and puncturing the bottle. It was a wonderful sight, though, shells bursting all round and above the yard, and the horses in the limbers standing as quiet as on parade. They are the most wonderful beasts . . .

Went to lunch at Brigade Headquarters with the C.O., but as the château was itself being shelled to hell by this time, we were both naturally anxious that it should clear up. By 12.30 rain had stopped and shelling decreased, so we set off for lunch. The trenches were really lovely after the rain, the grass, flowers and poppies being simply perfect. It was very quaint to see the C.O.'s orderly marching along in front of us in his tin hat, carrying every death-dealing appliance possible on his person, and holding in one swinging hand at his side a bright crimson poppy just sparkling with rain. This war is really a grotesque business. There is simply no sense in it . . .

My Bearer Sergeant is priceless on these occasions. (*They have just dealt with the results of sudden shelling.*) He is entirely unaffected by shelling, and walks round usually with his tin hat on the back of his neck like a sunbonnet; and to see him bandaging a man with a candle in the same hand as the bandage and spraying grease in every direction is a perfect treat to me. We got them all cleared off by about 4.30, and I went to bed and slept till 11, when my servant brought me some tea and biscuits, and a bright clean sun was pouring in through my door. It's always impossible to believe in the morning that one has had such a hell of a night. The country here is so green and full of flowers, and so quiet and peaceful in the mornings, that it is only by the new brown shell-holes and the colour of the water in my basin that I can believe that it really did take place.

Rode into Divisional Headquarters after tea. It was a lovely evening, and the ride through the rich cornfields ablaze with poppies was really beautiful. As we passed the crossroads there were four horses lying by the roadside. A shell had hit them a few minutes before I arrived; and there they lay, their poor feet thrown out awkwardly and their lips curled back to show their grey-green teeth in their death-agony. My own horse went past them with his head sideways and his ears working like semaphores ... I rode on down through the forest, the path looking beautiful, dappled with sunlight through the trees, and every now and again passing through little clouds of dancing flies, while in the ditches sometimes an early frog would croak. As we came out into the open again a Boche plane brought down an observation balloon in flames, and was himself shot down within a minute by one of our planes, which seemed to appear from nowhere. There was a group of five balloons close together and it was quaint to see the observers from all of them leave by parachute as one man, while the balloons themselves were hauled down like things in a child's toy theatre. I got back to camp about eight o'clock and changed for dinner ...

Maintaining its delicate balance between horror and poetry the diary continues until its writer is invalided out of the army shortly before the Armistice of 1918. In the Envoi to his book he sums up:

... So ended an unforgettable experience; and it is curious, in retrospect, to find how much one had enjoyed it. One had shared a common task with men of every type and station, and had been admitted therefore to a fellowship and intimacy so rare as to outweigh even the beastliness which made it possible. The tragedy of the war is not that so many lives were lost, but that this intimacy and fellowship – bought with so much agony and tears – should have been lost to the world in the end ... We are all where we were before – speaking a strange tongue one to another, and suspecting and guarding against an animosity which does not exist. We are no longer sharing a common burden, but bitterly competing one with another for a purse for our own advancement; and an enmity formerly reserved for Germans must therefore now include the man next door. And that I suppose is the truth of it – that only in mutual service lies the real hope of mankind.

Arnold Bennett, 1867–1931

Arnold Bennett was above all else a professional: whatever he had chosen to do he would have been as thorough and therefore probably as successful. It may seem self-evident that any writer who has his books published and paid for must be a professional; but there is a distinction that amounts to a great gaping void between him and the second writer whose diary is quoted here – Virginia Woolf. Bennett's professionalism displayed itself in many ways, but most interestingly perhaps in the accounts he kept of his output. At the end of every year he noted down how many hundred thousand words he had spun out of himself in the preceding twelve months. This curious weighing and measuring seems to come from another sphere altogether from the one in which Virginia Woolf agonised over her writing.

Virginia Woolf was born into an assured cultural background. Arnold Bennett came from a modest society and made his way into a vastly affluent one. He seemed able to turn his hand to every form of writing, and produced novels, plays, short stories and articles by the hundred. Shaw, Wells, Bennett – this is an inevitably quoted trio of names from the literary scene in the first years of this century. Bennett was a brilliant story-teller and the best of his work is not likely to be lost; *Tales of the Five Towns, The Card,* most of all *The Old Wives' Tale* stand on their own merit.

Arnold Bennett kept a journal from the year 1896, when he completed his first novel, until shortly before he died in 1931. The early volumes of the

Journals are freer and more consciously *written* than the later ones, which sometimes lapse into a kind of personal shorthand and a good deal of triviality. There is no doubt that they paint a portrait, by no means always a flattering one; in fact, it is hard to believe there was not a great deal more to the author of *The Old Wives' Tale* than he is prepared to admit to his diary. A final volume, self-edited, proves that he saw publication ahead by then, which may account for the sparser style. The professional's eye is on his readers, perhaps.

Once again, the social picture presented is an intensely interesting one. The years between the two wars as experienced by Arnold Bennett are packed with events which seem now quite of another world. There is so much entertainment and entertaining, so many telegrams, such gambling in glittering casinos. And the post-war dancing craze – a phenomenon we have almost forgotten – when the *palais de danse* was invented, and it was the thing to go to *thés dansants* in fashionable hotels. These years, too, might be called the last years of the man-about-town, the frequenter of exclusively male clubs, and restaurant dinners from which the womenfolk were excluded as a matter of course.

The extracts chosen here are mostly from the 1920s, particularly concerned with the theatre which, at this time, began to move towards realism, at first largely personified by Tchehov. As playwright and critic, Arnold Bennett's interests were increasingly bound up with the London theatre, from which he derived a large part of his income. The '20s extracts seem to fit quite snugly between one or two much earlier entries and one of the last.

The Journals of Arnold Bennett, 1896–1929

1896

April 27th

A fire engine was trotting down Chandos St. and in front of it two women in a victoria excitedly implored their coachman to draw to one side of the road. I walked on, and then, guessing that the fire must be near at hand, turned round, and hurrying as others hurried found myself at the edge of a loosely packed crowd in Villiers Street.

Three fire brigade vehicles, two of them steamers, and all three pair-horsed, were standing in line. Smoke and steam curled out idly from the glittering brass funnels of the steamers; the firemen talked and laughed in groups, unconcerned; and one or two idlers stroked the glossy flanks of the magnificent grey horses. No sign of a fire anywhere!

Then I saw people turning in under one of the arches beneath Charing Cross Station and I went to explore further . . . Beyond doubt the outbreak had been successfully dealt with before the engines arrived . . . A fire under Charing Cross Station might have proved a brilliant and exciting event, if circumstances had given it a chance . . .

Friday, May 15th
At noon precisely I finished my first novel, which was begun about the middle of April last year; but five-sixths of the work at least has been performed since the 1st October. Yesterday, I sat down at 3 p.m. to write, and, with slight interruptions for meals etc., kept at it till 1 a.m. this morning. The concluding chapter was written between 9 and 12 to-day.

My fears about 'In the Shadow' are (1) that it is not well-knit, (2) that it is hysterical, or at any rate strained in tone. Still, I should not be surprised if it impressed many respectable people . . .

Thursday, May 28th
John Lane (*the publisher*) showed me John Buchan's report on my novel. It was laudatory and kind, but not (I thought) critically appreciative. He had no fault whatever to find with the novel *qua* novel, but he said it would probably not be popular and that the same sort of thing had often been done before. Although it probably will not be popular, the same sort of thing has not been often done before; it has never been done before – in England . . . Lane said 'I will publish it,' and I said, 'That is very good of you,' or something like that, and that was really all that passed in the matter of the book . . .

1899

Sunday, December 31st
This year I have written 335,340 words, grand total. 288 articles and stories (including 4 instalments of a serial of 30,000–7,500 words each) have actually been published.

Also my book of plays – 'Polite Farces'.

I have written six or eight short stories not yet published or sold.

Also the greater part of a 55,000 word serial – 'Love and Life' – for Tillotsons, which begins publication about April next year. Also the whole draft (80,000 words) of my Staffordshire novel 'Anna Tellwright'.

My total earnings were £592.3.1d of which sum I have yet to receive £72.10s.

1907

Tuesday, December 31

I spent just over 23,000 frs. this year, and earned about 32,000 frs. I wrote 'The Statue' (with E.P.) and 'Sole Survivors' (with E.P.), 'Love and Riches', 'Death of Simon Fuge'. Five other short stories. First part of 'The Old Wives' Tale'. About 46 newspaper articles. And my journal. Also my play 'Cupid and Commonsense', and scenario of a new humorous novel, 'The Case of Leek'. Grand total: 375,000 words. This constitutes a record year.

1908

December 31st

... I have never worked so hard as this year, and I have not earned less for several years. But I have done fewer sillier things than usual.

I wrote 'Buried Alive', ¾ of 'The Old Wives' Tale', 'What the Public Wants', 'The Human Machine', 'Literary Taste: How to form it'; about half a dozen short stories, including 'A Matador in the Five Towns'; over sixty newspaper articles.

Total words, 423,500.

1922

It is not altogether surprising to find Arnold Bennett, by this time, holidaying in the Mediterranean with yacht-owning friends:

Amaryllis, Monte Carlo, Sunday, January 8th

At night, I was invited by Mrs. X. to dine at Ciro's. A good, nicely decorated, *chic* resturant and food good, but the dinner was awful , , ,

Amaryllis, Monte Carlo, Monday, January 9th
No novel yesterday. Saturday night I danced so much and heard
so much jazz band – the tunes ran through my head in bed and I
danced in bed – simple fatigue.

Amaryllis, Nice, Friday January 12th
Wednesday morning last dancing lesson from Pauline. I gave a
dance tea at the Park Palace, having written 1000 words. Yesterday we left Monaco harbour at 9.30 . . .

1924

Thursday, January 17th
. . . First night of 'Havoc', Haymarket. (*An early play about the
1914–18 war.*) Two fair acts (2 and 3) in which were only men,
and two other acts (1 and 4) dominated by women and a con-
ventional West End actor, namely Henry Kendall. Enormous
applause all through, numberless curtains, speeches, and yet I
can't see how this play can run. War acts fairly realistic in details
and solidities, but not in their main actions; so realistic in detail as
to be unpleasant to me; not beautiful . . . Mrs Leslie Faber (her
husband the star of the night) applauding like anything and she
and a few others keeping the applause alive when it ought to have
been dead . . .

Friday, February 8th
Last night, 1st performance of 'The Way of the World' at Lyric,
Hammersmith. I have seen two rehearsals and the performance of
this play, and still do not know what the plot is, nor have I met
anyone who does know . . . The performance and production last
night were admirable. The play will fail, but it must add to the
prestige of the theatre. Edith Evans as Millamant gave the finest
comedy performance I have ever seen on the stage. I went behind
afterwards, told her so. 'How exciting!' she said.

Monday, February 11th
Last night, Fellowship of Players performance of 'Macbeth' at
Strand Theatre with Beatrice Wilson and Edmund Willard as
principals. Arthur Bourchier was asked to speak a few words 'to

begin with'. Speech called for at the end. Milton (*the producer*) made it. It ended thus: 'Whatever is good in the production is the players', whatever is bad is the producer's'. 'No, no!' protests from the stage, etc. More applause. Why will stage people do these things? God knoweth. It was all so characteristic and so childish, and so 'stagey'.

Tuesday, February 19th

D. and I to first night playing of 'Back to Methuselah' last night at Court Theatre. 'House full' boards outside before the performance ... I was very bored by the play, I could see nothing in it; neither action nor character nor a sermon nor wit ... A most depressing night.

Saturday, May 10th

I saw Sir Edward Elgar at the Garrick the other day. I said I was working hard. He at once said, 'Ah, you work because it pleases you; we poor men work because we have to.' He seldom talks to me without mentioning his poverty and my riches ...

Tuesday, May 13th

Yesterday after lunch I went with L. Faber to Haymarket to meet Hilda Trevelyan, etc., at rehearsal of 'Great Adventure'. (*This was the dramatised version of Bennett's novel* Buried Alive) ... Enclosed stage, curtain down, etc. Very, very small after Drury Lane ... This theatre seems to be a sort of enclosed ring, which no one can enter save by permission. Old courtesy is preserved here and cleanliness reigns. At the stage entrance is a card, and written on it (ought to have been printed): 'Please wipe your boots.' I have never seen this before at a stage-door ...

Tuesday, June 10th

I went to the 'Great Adventure' at the Haymarket on Saturday night for the 2nd act only, in order to see what Ilam Carve was doing during Honoria's long speech in Sc. 2. describing the funeral. I found that the star was playing the fool and getting laughs the whole time, drawing the attention of the audience away from the speech and preventing it from getting over. So I

wrote to him to try to stop this. He was, like many stars, flag-
rantly breaking a rule which he would lay down for every other
member of the cast.

Tuesday June 17th
Elsa Lanchester and Harold Scott came to lunch yesterday. She
had a most charming dress, home-made. She said she had made it
out of dusters, and I believe she had . . .

1925

Wednesday 4th February
'The Vortex' by Noel Coward, Royalty Theatre . . . This play
has made a great stir. First Act played 43 minutes, and the first
half-hour, and more, was spent in merely creating an atmosphere.
Talk whose direction you couldn't follow. No fair hint of plot
till nearly the end – and hardly even then . . . In 2nd Act some
tiny glimpses of dramatic talent and ingenuities . . . Coward plays
the son well, and Lilian Braithwaite gets through the mother as a
sort of *tour de force* . . . Some smartness in the play, and certainly
the germs of an effective dramatic skill; but really I saw nothing
that was *true* except in minor details. I dozed off once in the last
Act . . .

Monday, June 22nd
On Saturday I returned from 17 days' yachting. Not two minutes' rain in the whole time. (*His own yacht, by now.*)
     Tonight 'The Cherry Orchard' is transferred from the Lyric,
Hammersmith, to the Royalty. This I think marks a definite turn
in public taste towards true plays. I have been remarking this
turn for some years, but managers seem to be quite blind to it . . .
Tonight this most disconcerting and original play is going in a
sort of triumph to the West End, where no manager would have
looked at it a month ago . . .

Wednesday, June 24th
. . . The revival of 'The Beggar's Opera' last night at the Lyric,
Hammersmith, was an affair of *prodigious enthusiasm*, and well
done in some ways. Here is an absolutely English thing, under-

stood by English artists, and done by them excellently well so far as the limitations of their gifts would allow. The music is lovely, heavenly sometimes, and the dialogue always brilliant. Also it is daring and bawdy, with robust ideas about life. This is in my opinion one of the most wonderful entertainments I have ever seen.

Arnold Bennett's running commentary on the London theatre continues over the next few years, for he was increasingly involved, as critic and author. His journal for 1929 has been selected and worked over by himself, and from this it seems interesting to extract one 'generation-gap' entry which needs little alteration to have been written today:

London, December 12th
If a set of young men from the East End or from some provincial centre of Association football had gone in mass formation to Twickenham Football ground last Monday and by force and rowdyism rendered impossible the playing of the inter-Varsity match, there would have been a loud outcry in the papers, and in all polite circles, against their ill-mannered lawlessness ...

Yet such conduct would have been no worse than the conduct, on that same day, of undergraduates from our ancient universities, which conduct began with processions on the tops of dining-tables in fashionable restaurants and ended in the breaking up of a performance in at least one West End theatre; and which conduct occupied only a few inches of space in the papers and was forgotten by an enlightened public in less than twenty-four hours. It was generally understood that University rowdyism in London had been finished for ever by certain outrageous, destructive antics last year. Not so.

The proof of the pudding is in the eating. If years of education at public schools and universities result in exhibitions of loutish violence which have no equal in Great Britain, what are we to think of the real value of such education? Whatever young men are taught at universities, they are not effectively taught either decency or good manners or self-control or self-respect for the elementary social rights of others. They are taught to behave like savages – and to be proud of it. The immediate cause of these disgraces is, of course, simple drunkenness, senseless and brutish indulgence in alcohol. The excuse offered for the youths is that they are young. Which plainly implies a theory that we ought not to expect citizens to be decent, civilised and law-abiding until they have reached the age of at least twenty-one. Is this a tenable theory?

Virginia Woolf, 1882–1941

Virginia Woolf was a writer who came into enormous prominence during the 1920s and 30s. In her novels she used the 'stream of consciousness' or 'interior monologue', the characters' innermost thoughts forming an integral part of the narrative. Her style may seem now over-elaborate, but it has made an indelible mark on the writing of English fiction. Her best-known novels are *Mrs Dalloway*, *To the Lighthouse*, *The Waves* and *The Years*.

Virginia Woolf and her husband, Leonard, were members of a coterie of intellectuals who came to be known as the Bloomsbury Group. This group embraced many famous names, among them E. M. Forster and Lytton Strachey. The Woolfs founded a publishing house, 'The Hogarth Press', and for a time did all the printing themselves. The press flourished and became famous for its distinguished publications. Later, the Woolfs lived in Sussex, near Lewes. It was here in 1941 that Virginia, who all her life had suffered depressive mental illness, drowned herself in the River Ouse.

A Writer's Diary is edited by Leonard Woolf. The extracts chosen here all relate to her work, for this is above all else a worker's notebook.

A Writer's Diary, 1918–1941

1919

Thursday, March 27th (Leonard Woolf has just read a completed manuscript of the novel called Night and Day.)

... I own that his verdict, finally pronounced this morning, gives me immense pleasure: how far one should discount it, I don't know. In my own opinion N. & D. is a much more mature and finished and satisfactory book than *The Voyage Out*; as it has reason to be. I suppose I lay myself open to the charge of niggling with emotions that don't really matter. I certainly don't anticipate even two editions. And yet I can't help thinking, English fiction being what it is, I compare for originality and sincerity rather well with most of the moderns. L. finds the philosophy very melancholy. It too much agrees with what he was saying yesterday. Yet, if one is to deal with people on a large scale and say what one thinks, how can one avoid melancholy? I don't admit to being hopeless, though: only the spectacle is a profoundly strange one; and as the current answers don't do, one has to grope for a new one, and the process of discarding the old, when one is by no means certain what to put in their place, is a sad one. Still, if you think of it, what answers do Arnold Bennett or Thackeray, for instance, suggest? Happy ones — satisfactory solutions — answers one would accept, if one had the least respect for one's soul? Now I have done my last odious piece of typewriting, and when I have scribbled this page, I shall write and suggest Monday as a day for coming up to lunch with Gerald (*Duckworth, her publisher and half-brother*). I don't suppose I've ever enjoyed any writing so much as I did the last half of *Night and Day*. Indeed, no part of it taxed me as *The Voyage Out* did; and if one's own ease and interest promise anything good, I should have hopes that some people, at least, will find it a pleasure. I wonder if I shall ever be able to read it again? Is the time coming when I can endure to read my own writing in print without blushing — shivering and wishing to take cover?

K

1921

Thursday, August 18*th (She is ill.)*
Nothing to record; only an intolerable fit of the fidgets to write away. Here I am chained to my rock; forced to do nothing; doomed to let every worry, spite, irritation and obsession scratch and claw and come again. This is a day that I may not walk and must not work. Whatever book I read bubbles up in my mind as part of an article I want to write. No one in the whole of Sussex is so miserable as I am; or so conscious of an infinite capacity of enjoyment hoarded in me, could I use it. The sun streams (no, never streams; floods rather) down upon all the yellow fields and the long low barns; and what wouldn't I give to be coming through Firle woods, dirty and hot, with my nose turned home, every muscle tired and the brains laid up in sweet lavender, so sane and cool, and ripe for the morrow's task. How I should notice everything – the phrase for it coming the moment after and fitting like a glove; and then on the dusty road as I ground my pedals, so my story would begin telling itself; and home, and some bout of poetry after dinner, half read, half lived, as if the flesh were dissolved and through it the flowers burst red and white. There! I've written out half my irritation, I hear poor L. driving the lawn mower up and down, for a wife like I am should have a latch to her cage. She bites! And he spent all yesterday running round London for me. Still if one is Prometheus, if the rock is hard and the gadflies pungent, gratitude, affection, none of the nobler feelings have sway. And so this August is wasted . . .

1927

Wednesday, June 22*nd*
Women haters depress me and both Tolstoi and Mrs Asquith hate women. I suppose my depression is a form of vanity. But then so are all strong opinions on both sides. I hate Mrs A.'s hard dogmatic empty style. But enough: I shall write about her tomorrow. I write every day about something and have deliberately set apart a few weeks to money-making, so that I may put £50 in each of our pockets by September. This will

be the first money of my own since I married. I never feel the need of it lately. And I can get it, if I want it, but shirk writing for money.

Sunday, November 20th
I will now snatch a moment from what Morgan (*E. M. Forster*) calls 'life' to enter a hurried note. My notes have been few; life a cascade, a glissade, a torrent; all together. I think on the whole this *is* our happiest autumn. So much work; and success now; and life on easy terms; heaven knows what. My morning rushes, pell mell, from 10 to 1. I write so quick I can't get it typed before lunch . . .

1930

Wednesday August 20th
The Waves is I think resolving itself (am at page 100) into a series of dramatic soliloquies. The thing is to keep them running homogeneously in and out, in the rhythm of the waves. Can they be read consecutively? I know nothing about that. I think this is the greatest opportunity I have yet been able to give myself; therefore I suppose the most complete failure. Yet I respect myself for writing this book – yes – even though it exhibits my congenital faults.

Tuesday, December 2nd (At a party given by a friend she meets Arnold Bennett.)
. . . There I was for 2 hours so it seemed, alone with B. in Ethel's little back room. And this meeting I am convinced was engineered by B. to 'get on good terms with Mrs Woolf' – when Heaven knows I don't care a rap if I'm on terms with B. or not . . . He ceases; shuts his eyes; leans back; one waits. 'Begin' he at last articulates quietly, without any fluster. But the method lengthens out intolerably a rather uninspired discourse. It's fun. I like the old creature. I do my best, as a writer, to detect signs of genius in his smoky brown eye: I see certain sensuality, power, I suppose . . .
'It's the only life,' he said (this incessant scribbling, one word after another, one thousand words daily). 'I don't want anything else. I think of nothing but writing. Some people are bored.' 'You

have all the clothes you want, I suppose,' I said. 'And bath. And bed. And a yacht.' 'Oh yes, my clothes couldn't be better cut.' ... 'And you drop your aitches on purpose,' I said, 'thinking that you possess more "life" than we do.' 'I sometimes tease,' said B., 'but I don't think I possess more life than you do. Now I must go home. I have to write one thousand words tomorrow morning.' And this left only the scrag end of the evening; and this left me in a state where I can hardly drive my pen across the page ...

1931

Monday, August 17th
Well now, it being just after 12.30, I have put the last corrections in *The Waves*; done my proofs; and they shall go tomorrow — never, never to be looked at again by me, I imagine.

Monday, October 5th
A note to say I am all trembling with pleasure — can't get on with my Letter — because Harold Nicholson has rung up to say *The Waves* is a masterpiece. Ah Hah — so it wasn't all wasted then ...

Friday, October 9th
Really, this unintelligible book is being better 'received' than any of them. A note in *The Times* proper — the first time this has been allowed me. And it sells — how unexpected, how odd that people can read that difficult grinding stuff!

1933

Wednesday, May 31st
I think I have now got to the point where I can write for four months straight ahead at *The Pargiters*. (*Later called* The Years.) Oh the relief — the physical relief! I feel as if I could hardly any longer keep back — that my brain is being tortured by always butting against a blank wall ... The thing is to be venturous, bold, to take every possible fence. One might introduce plays, poems, letters, dialogues; must get the round, not only the flat. Not the theory only. And conversation: argument. How to do that will be one of the problems. I mean intellectual argument in the form of art: I mean how give ordinary waking Arnold Ben-

nett life the form of art? These rich hard problems for my four months ahead . . .

1937

Saturday, 20th February

I turn my eyes away from the Press as I go upstairs, because there are all the review copies of *The Years* packed and packing. They go out next week: this is my last weekend of comparative peace. What do I anticipate with such clammy coldness? I think chiefly that my friends won't mention it; will turn the conversation rather awkwardly. I think I anticipate considerable lukewarmness among the friendly reviewers – respectful tepidity; and a whoop of Red Indian delight from the Grigs who will joyfully and loudly announce that this is the longdrawn twaddle of a prim prudish bourgeois mind, and say that now no one can take Mrs W. seriously again . . .

Friday, 12 *March*

Oh the relief! L. brought the *Lit. Sup.* to me in bed and said It's quite good. And so it is; and *Time and Tide* says I'm a first rate novelist and a great lyrical poet. And I can already hardly read through the reviews: but feel a little dazed, to think then it's *not* nonsense; it does make an effect. Yet of course not in the least the effect I meant. But now, my dear, after all that agony, I'm free, whole; round: can go full ahead. And so stop this cry of content and sober joy . . . I have once more loaded myself with the strain of *Three Guineas*, at which I have been writing hard and laboriously. So now I'm straining to draw that cart across the rough ground. It seems therefore that there is no rest; no sense of It's finished. One always harnesses oneself by instinct; and can't live without the strain. Now *The Years* will completely die out from my mind . . .

1939

Monday, August 7

. . . Oh and I thought, as I was dressing, how interesting it would be to describe the approach of age, and the gradual coming of death. As people describe love. To note every symptom of failure:

but why failure? To treat age as an experience that is different from others; and to detect every one of the gradual stages towards death which is a tremendous experience, and not as unconscious, at least in its approaches, as birth is. I must now return to my grind, I think rather refreshed.

Wednesday, August 9th
My grind has left me dazed and depressed. How on earth to bring off this chapter? God knows.

Wednesday, September 6th
... This war has begun in cold blood. One merely feels that the killing machine has to be set in action ... I conceived the idea, walking in the sunbaked marsh where I saw one clouded yellow, of making an article out of these 15 odd diaries ... But shall I ever have a few hours to read in?

1940

Monday, May 13
I admit to some content, some closing of a chapter and peace comes with it, from posting my proofs today. I admit – because we're in the third day of 'the greatest battle in history'. It began (here) with the 8 o'clock wireless announcing as I lay half asleep the invasion of Holland and Belgium ... So my little moment of peace comes in a yawning hollow ...

1941

Sunday, March 8th
... I mark Henry James's sentence: observe perpetually. Observe the oncome of age. Observe greed. Observe my own despondency. By that means it becomes serviceable. Or so I hope. I insist upon spending this time to the best advantage. I will go down with my colours flying. This I see verges on introspection; but doesn't quite fall in. Suppose I bought a ticket at the Museum; biked in daily and read history. Suppose I selected one dominant figure in every age and wrote round and about. Occupation is essential. And now with some pleasure I find that it's seven; and must cook dinner. Haddock and sausage meat. I think it is true that one

gains a certain hold on sausage and haddock by writing them down.

With this entry A Writer's Diary *comes to an end. Three weeks later Virginia Woolf was dead.*

The Diary of a Nobody

GEORGE GROSSMITH & WEEDON GROSSMITH

It seems fair to include fictional diaries among the rest. *The Diary of a Nobody* was published in 1892 and it has become a classic. Its writer and hero, Mr Pooter, lives on the outskirts of London and works as a clerk in the City. He has a devoted wife, Carrie, and one son. This young man, always known as Willie, suddenly announces his intention to be called by his middle name, Lupin. He has grown a bit of a 'swell' in the course of his employment at a bank in the North. 'He asked for a drop of brandy with a sort of careless look,' his father records, 'which to my mind was theatrical and quite ineffective.'

Probably nobody else in the world before or since has been called Lupin; but all the names are splendid in this book. Mr Pooter says to a visitor: 'If you like to stay, Mr Fosselton, for our usual crust – pray do.' He replied: 'Oh! thanks; but please call me Burwin-Fosselton. It is a double name. There are lots of Fosseltons, but please call me Burwin-Fosselton.'

Mr Pooter has something in common with Thomas Turner of East Hoathly. Both are in a modest way of business, concerned with family matters, easily offended and socially anxious. The difference, of course, lies in the fact that Thomas Turner was a real person, while Charley Pooter is the invention of his author. This puts Mr Pooter at a disadvantage, for *his* creator is laughing at him.

*   *   *

'My dear wife Carrie and I,' writes Mr Pooter, 'have just been a week in our new house, "The Laurels", Brickfield Terrace, Holloway – a nice six-roomed residence, not counting basement, with a front breakfast-parlour. We have a little front garden; and there is a flight of ten steps up to the front door, which, by-the-by, we keep locked with the chain up ... We have a nice little back garden which runs down to the railway. We were rather afraid of the noise of the trains at first, but the landlord said we should not notice them after a bit, and took £2 off the rent. He was certainly right; and beyond the cracking of the garden wall at the bottom, we have suffered no inconvenience ... After my work in the City, I like to be at home ... There is always something to be done: a tin-tack here, a Venetian blind to be put straight, a fan to nail up or part of a carpet to nail down – all of which I can do with my pipe in my mouth; while Carrie is not above putting a button on a shirt, mending a pillow-case, or practising the "Sylvia Gavotte" on our new cottage piano ... It is also a great comfort to us to know that our boy Willie is getting on so well in the Bank at Oldham. We should like to see more of him. Now for my diary:'

April 8th (Sunday)
After Church, the Curate came back with us. I sent Carrie in to open the front door, which we do not use except on special occasions. She could not get it open and after all my display, I had to take the Curate (whose name, by-the-by, I did not catch) round the side entrance. He caught his foot in the scraper, and tore the bottom of his trousers. Most annoying, as Carrie could not well offer to repair them on a Sunday. After dinner, went to sleep. Took a walk round the garden and discovered a beautiful spot for sowing mustard-and-cress and radishes. Went to Church again in the evening: walked back with the Curate. Carrie noticed he had got on the same pair of trousers, only repaired. He wants me to take round the plate, which I think a great compliment.

April 10th
... It is disgraceful how late some of the young clerks are arriving. I told three of them that if Mr Perkupp, the principal, heard of it, they might be discharged.

Pitt, a monkey of seventeen, who has only been with us six weeks, told me 'to keep my hair on!' I informed him I had had the honour of being in the firm twenty years, to which he insolently replied that I 'looked it'. I gave him an indignant look, and said: 'I demand from you some respect, sir.' He replied: 'All right, go on demanding.' You cannot argue with people like that. In the evening Gowing called (*he is a neighbour of the Pooters'; Cummings is another; they treat Mr Pooter abominably*) and repeated his complaint about the smell of paint. Gowing is sometimes very tedious with his remarks, and not always cautious; and Carrie once very properly reminded him that she was present.

April 11*th*
Mustard-and-cress and radishes not come up yet. Today was a day of annoyances. I missed the quarter-to-nine bus to the City, through having words with the grocer's boy, who for the second time had the impertinence to bring his basket to the hall-door, and left the marks of his dirty boots on the fresh-cleaned door-steps ... I was half-an-hour late at the office, a thing that has never happened to me before... Mr Perkupp, our principal, unfortunately chose this very morning to pounce down upon us early ... As I passed by Pitt's desk, I heard him remark to his neighbour: 'How disgracefully late some of the head clerks arrive!' This was, of course, meant for me. I treated the observation with silence, simply giving him a look, which unfortunately had the effect of making both of the clerks laugh. Thought afterwards it would have been more dignified if I had pretended not to have heard him at all. Cummings called in the evening, and we played dominoes.

April 12*th*
Mustard-and-cress and radishes not come up yet ... In the evening, after tea, Gowing dropped in ... Gowing began his usual sniffing, so, anticipating him, I said: 'You're not going to complain of the smell of paint again?' He said: 'No, not this time; but I'll tell you what, I distinctly smell dry rot.' I don't often make jokes, but I replied: 'You're talking a lot of *dry rot* yourself.' I could not help roaring at this, and Carrie said her sides quite

ached with laughter. I never was so immensely tickled by anything I had ever said before. I actually woke up twice during the night, and laughed till the bed shook.

At the end of April, the Pooters receive an invitation to the Lord Mayor's ball at the Mansion House to 'meet the Representatives of Trades and Commerce'. It would be foolish to attempt an extract; this chapter should be read in full. In August, Pooter Junior comes home unexpectedly:

August 5th (Sunday)
We have not seen Willie since last Christmas, and are pleased to notice what a fine young man he has grown. One would scarcely believe he was Carrie's son. He looks more like a younger brother. I rather disapprove of his wearing a check suit on a Sunday, and I think he ought to have gone to church this morning; but he said he was tired after yesterday's journey, so I refrained from any remark on the subject. We had a bottle of port for dinner, and drank dear Willie's health.

He said: 'Oh, by-the-by, did I tell you I've cut my first name, William, and taken the second name, Lupin? In fact, I'm only known at Oldham as Lupin Pooter. If you were to Willie me there, they wouldn't know what you meant.'

Of course, Lupin being a purely family name, Carrie was delighted, and began by giving a long history of the Lupins. I ventured to say that I thought William a nice simple name, and reminded him he was christened after his Uncle William, who was much respected in the City. Willie, in a manner I did not much care for, said sneeringly: 'Oh, I know all about that – Good old Bill!' and helped himself to a third glass of port.

Carrie objects strongly to my saying 'Good old', but she made no remark when Willie used the double adjective. I said nothing, but looked at her, which meant more. I said: 'My dear Willie, I hope you are happy with your colleagues at the Bank.' He replied: 'Lupin, if you please; and with respect to the Bank, there's not a clerk who is a gentleman, and the "boss" is a cad.' I felt so shocked, I could say nothing, and my instinct told me there was something wrong.

Next morning, Lupin stays in bed and does not appear until nearly three o'clock:

August 6th (Bank Holiday)
... I said: 'We have not seen much of you, and you will have to return by the 5.30 train; therefore you will have to leave in an hour, unless you go by the midnight mail.' He said: 'Look here, Guv'nor, it's no use beating about the bush. I've tendered my resignation at the Bank.'

For a moment I could not speak. When my speech came again, I said: 'How dare you, sir? How dare you take such a serious step without consulting me? Don't answer me, sir! — you will sit down immediately, and write a note at my dictation, withdrawing your resignation and amply apologising for your thoughtlessness.'

Imagine my dismay when he replied with a loud guffaw: 'It's no use. If you want the good old truth, I've got the chuck!'

After several unfortunate attempts, Mr Pooter finds Lupin a job through the kind offices of his boss, Mr Perkupp. Lupin falls madly in love with a girl called Daisy Mutlar, and the Pooters give a party:

November 15th
A red-letter day. Our first important party since we have been in this house. I got home early from the City. Lupin insisted on having a hired waiter, and stood a half-dozen of champagne. I think this is an unnecessary expense, but Lupin said he had had a piece of luck, having made three pounds out of a private deal in the City. I hope he won't gamble in his new situation. The supper-room looked so nice, and Carrie truly said: 'We need not be ashamed of its being seen by Mr Perkupp, should he honour us by coming.'

I dressed early in case people should arrive punctually at eight o'clock, and was much vexed to find my new dress-trousers much too short. Lupin, who is getting beyond his position, found fault with my wearing ordinary boots instead of dress-boots.

I replied satirically: 'My dear son, I have lived to be above that sort of thing.'

Lupin burst out laughing, and said: 'A man generally was above his boots.'

This may be funny or it may *not;* but I was gratified to find he had not discovered the coral had come off one of my studs. Carrie looked a picture, wearing the dress she wore at the Mansion House. The arrangement of the drawing-room was excellent. Carrie had hung muslin curtains over the folding-doors, and also over one of the entrances, for we had removed the door from its hinges . . .

The first arrival was Gowing, who, with his usual taste, greeted me with: 'Hulloh, Pooter, why your trousers are too short!'

I simply said: 'Very likely, and you will find my temper *short* also.'

He said: 'That won't make your trousers longer, Juggins. You should get your missus to put a flounce on them.'

I wonder I waste my time entering his insulting observations in my diary . . .

Carrie and I were rather startled at Daisy's appearance. She had a bright-crimson dress on, cut very low in the neck. I do not think such a style modest. She ought to have taken a lesson from Carrie and covered her shoulders with a little lace . . .

We had some music, and Lupin, who never left Daisy's side for a moment, raved over her singing of a song, called 'Some Day'. It seemed a pretty song, but she made such grimaces, and sang, to my mind, so out of tune, I would not have asked her to sing again; but Lupin made her sing four songs right off, one after the other.

At ten o'clock we went down to supper, and from the way Gowing and Cummings ate you would have thought they had not had a meal for a month. I told Carrie to keep something back in case Mr Perkupp should come by mere chance. Gowing annoyed me by filling a large tumbler of champagne, and drinking it straight off. He repeated the action and made me fear our half-dozen of champagne would not last out. I tried to keep a bottle back, but Lupin got hold of it, and took it to the side-table with Daisy and Frank Mutlar (*her brother*).

We went upstairs, and the young fellows began skylarking. Carrie put a stop to that at once . . . I did not notice that Lupin and Frank had disappeared. I asked Mr Watson ... where they were and he said: 'It's a case of "Oh, what a surprise!"'

We were directed to form a circle – which we did. Watson then said: 'I have much pleasure in introducing the celebrated Blondin Donkey.' Frank and Lupin then bounded into the room. Lupin had whitened his face like a clown, and Frank had tied round his waist a large hearthrug. He was supposed to be the donkey, and he looked it. They indulged in a very noisy pantomime and we were all shrieking with laughter.

I turned round suddenly, and then I saw Mr Perkupp standing half-way in the door, he having arrived without our knowing it. I beckoned to Carrie and we went up to him at once. He would not come right into the room. I apologised for the foolery, but Mr Perkupp said: 'Oh, it seems amusing.' I could see he was not a bit amused.

Carrie and I took him downstairs, but the table was a wreck. There was not a glass of champagne left – not even a sandwich. Mr Perkupp said he required nothing, but would like a glass of seltzer or soda-water. The last syphon was empty. Carrie said: 'We have plenty of port wine left.' Mr Perkupp said, with a smile: 'No, thank you. I really require nothing, but I am most pleased to see you and your husband in your own home. Good-night, Mrs Pooter – you will excuse my very short stay, I know.' I went with him to his carriage, and he said: 'Don't trouble to come to the office till twelve to-morrow.'

I felt despondent as I went back into the house, and I told Carrie I thought the party was a failure. Carrie said it was a great success, and I was only tired, and insisted on my having some port myself. I drank two glasses and felt much better, and we went into the drawing-room, where they had commenced dancing. Carrie and I had a little dance, which I said reminded me of old days. She said I was a spooney old thing.

Although Mr Pooter is forever threatening to conclude his diary, because he is too disheartened by one snub or another to continue, something always turns up. A rise in salary – a compliment from Mr Perkupp – an invitation to a ball given by the East Acton Rifle Brigade . . . Lupin continues to distress and alarm, breaking one engagement only to embark on another. Eventually he announces his forthcoming marriage to Miss Lillie Posh, daughter of wealthy Murray Posh . . . This announcement coincides with a gesture from Mr Perkupp that fills Charley Pooter's cup to overflowing . . . And there The Diary of a Nobody *comes to a graceful conclusion.*

Diary of a Provincial Lady

E. M. DELAFIELD

The other fictional diary to be allowed into this collection was written from the masculine point of view and *Diary of a Provincial Lady* is its obvious partner. E. M. Delafield was a prolific and successful novelist of the '30s and '40s, but nothing she wrote had the immediate popularity of the *Provincial Lady*. This began as occasional pieces written for the weekly *Time and Tide*, but eventually extended into four volumes.

The Provincial Lady lives somewhere in the West Country, she shops in Plymouth or Exeter. She has a husband, Robert, concerned in some gentlemanly way with pigs and with Lady B., the lady of the manor; a son, Robin, away at prep school; a daughter, Vicky, with Mademoiselle to look after her; a cook, a house-parlourmaid, a gardener. Such a household would seem to leave plenty of time in hand. She seems, however, never to catch up with herself, money is scarce, Robert is taciturn – whenever cash is unexpectedly needed, she dashes to Plymouth and pawns her great-aunt's diamond ring.

The diary is always amusing and often really witty and is interesting, too, from a purely social point of view. The time of the first three books is immediately pre-war. The first book, from which the extracts here are taken, deals all unknowing with a way of life that had only a year or two more to run. When the war was over Provincial Ladies of this kind had completely disappeared. They had merged into another, far more embracing character, the classless British Housewife. This process may be observed in action in *The Provincial Lady in Wartime*.

In a genuine diary it is often the briefest entries that tell the most about the writer. In a fictional diary there are bound to be 'set pieces', and these are the most obvious choice for inclusion here.

*   *   *

The Provincial Lady and her family go on a picnic with a neighbour, Miss Pankerton, her two nephews and her two dogs.

August 15th
Picnic takes place under singular and rather disastrous conditions, day not beginning well owing to Robin and Henry (*a visiting schoolfriend*) having strange overnight inspiration about sleeping out in summer-house, which is prepared for them with much elaboration by Mademoiselle and myself—even to crowning touch from Mademoiselle of small vase of flowers on table. At 2 a.m. they decide that they wish to come in, and do so through study window left open for them. Henry involves himself in several blankets, which he tries to carry upstairs, and trips and falls down, and Robin knocks over hall-stool, and treads on Helen Wills (*the cat*).

Robert and myself are roused, and Robert is not pleased. Mademoiselle appears on landing in *peignoir* and with head swathed in little grey shawl, but screams at the sight of Robert in pyjamas, and rushes away again. (The French undoubtedly very curious mixture of modesty and the reverse.)

Henry and Robin show tendency to become explanatory, but are discouraged, and put into beds. Just as I return down passage to my room, sounds indicate that Vicky has now awakened, and is automatically opening campaign by saying Can't I come too? Instinct—unclassified, but evidently stronger than maternal one— bids me to leave Mademoiselle to deal with this, which I unhesitatingly do.

Get into bed again, feeling that the day has not opened very well, but sleep off and on until Gladys calls me—ten minutes late— but do not say anything about her unpunctuality, as Robert does not appear to have noticed it.

L

Sky is grey, but not necessarily threatening, and glass has not fallen unreasonably. All is in readiness when Miss Pankerton (wearing Burberry, green knitted cap, and immense yellow gloves) appears in large Ford car which brims over with nephews, sheep-dogs, and a couple of men. Latter resolve themselves into the Pankerton brother – who turns out to be from Vancouver – and the friend who Writes – very tall and pale, and is addressed by Miss P. in a proprietory manner as 'Jahsper'.

(Something tells me that Robert and Jahsper are not going to care about one another.)

After customary preliminaries about weather, much time is spent in discussing arrangements in cars. All the children show tendency to wish to sit with their own relations rather than anybody else, except Henry, who says simply that the hired car looks the best, and may he sit in front with the driver, please. All is greatly complicated by presence of sheep-dogs, and Robert offers to shut them into an outhouse for the day, but Miss Pankerton replies that this would break their hearts, bless them, and they can just pop down anywhere among the baskets. (In actual fact, both eventually pop down on Mademoiselle's feet, and she looks despairing, and presently asks if I have by any chance a little bottle of eau-de-Cologne with me – which I naturally haven't.)

Picnic baskets, as usual, weigh incredible amount, and Thermos flasks stick up at inconvenient angles and run into our legs. (I quote *John Gilpin* rather aptly, but nobody pays any attention.)

When we have driven about ten miles, rain begins, and goes on and on. Cars are stopped, and we find that two schools of thought exist, one – of which Miss P. is the leader – declaring that we are Running out of It, and the other – headed by the Vancouver brother and heavily backed by Robert – that we are Running into It. Miss P. – as might have been expected – wins, and we proceed; but Run into It more and more. By the time destination is reached, we have Run into It to an extent that makes me wonder if we shall ever Run out of It.

Lunch has to beea ten in three bathing huts, hired by Robert, and the children become hilarious and fidgety, Miss P. talks about companionate marriage to Robert, who makes no answer, and Jahsper asks me what I think of James Elroy Flecker. As I cannot remember exact form of J.E.F.'s activities, I merely reply that in many ways he was very wonderful – which no doubt he was – and Jahsper seems satisfied, and eats tomato sandwiches. The children ask riddles – mostly very old and foolish ones – and Miss P. looks annoyed, and says See if it has stopped raining – which it hasn't. I feel that she and the children must, at all costs, be kept apart, and tell Robert in urgent whisper that, rain or no rain, they must go out.

They do.

Miss Pankerton suddenly becomes expansive and remarks to Jahsper that *Now* he can see what she meant, about positively Victorian survivals to be found in English family life. At this, Vancouver brother looks aghast – as well he may – and dashes out into the wet. Jahsper says Yerse, Yerse, and sighs, and I at once institute vigorous search for missing plate, which creates a diversion.

Subsequently the children bathe, get wetter than ever, drip all over the place, and are dried – Mademoiselle predicts death from pneumonia for all – and we seek the cars once more. One sheep-dog is missing, but eventually recovered in soaking condition, and is gathered on to the united laps of Vicky, Henry, and a nephew. I lack energy to protest, and we drive away.

Beg Miss P., Jahsper, brother, nephews, sheep-dogs and all, to come in and get dry and have tea, but they have the decency to refuse and I make no further effort, but watch them depart with untold thankfulness.

(Should be sorry to think impulses of hospitality almost entirely dependent on convenience, but cannot altogether escape suspicion that this is so.)

Robert extremely forbearing on the whole, and says nothing worse than Well! – but this very expressively.

October 17th
Surprising invitation to evening party – Dancing, 9.30 – at Lady B.'s. Cannot possibly refuse, as Robert has been told to make himself useful there in various ways; moreover, entire neighbour-

hood is obviously being polished off, and see no object in raising question as to whether we have, or have not, received invitation. Decide to get new dress, but must have it made locally, owing to rather sharply worded enquiry from London shop which has the privilege of serving me, as to whether I have not overlooked overdue portion of account? (Far from overlooking it, have actually been kept awake by it at night.) Proceed to Plymouth, and get very attractive black taffeta, with little pink and blue posies scattered over it. Mademoiselle removes, and washes, Honiton lace from old purple velvet every-night teagown and assures me that it will be *gentil à croquer* on new taffeta. Also buy new pair black evening-shoes, but shall wear them every evening for at least an hour in order to ensure reasonable comfort at party.

Am able to congratulate myself that great-aunt's diamond ring, for once, is at home when needed.

Robert rather shatteringly remarks that he believes the dancing is only for the *young* people, and I heatedly enquire how line of demarcation is to be laid down? Should certainly not dream of accepting ruling from Lady B. on any such delicate question. Robert merely repeats that only the young will be *expected* to dance, and we drop the subject, and I enquire into nature of refreshments to be expected at party, half-past nine seems to me a singularly inhospitable hour, involving no regular meal whatever. Robert begs that I will order dinner at home exactly as usual, and make it as substantial as possible, so as to give him every chance of keeping awake at party, and I agree that this would indeed appear desirable.

October 19*th*

Rumour that Lady B.'s party is to be in Fancy Dress throws entire neighbourhood into consternation. Our Vicar's Wife comes down on gardener's wife's bicycle – borrowed, she says, for greater speed and urgency – and explains that, in her position, she does not think that fancy dress would do at all – unless perhaps *poudré*, which, she asserts, is different, but takes ages to brush out afterwards. She asks what I am going to do, but am quite unable to enlighten her, as black taffeta already completed. Mademoiselle,

at this, intervenes, and declares that black taffeta can be trans-
formed by a touch into Dresden China Shepherdess *à ravir*.
Am obliged to beg her not to be ridiculous, nor attempt to make
me so, and she then insanely suggests turning black taffeta into
costume for (*a*) Mary Queen of Scots, (*b*) Mme de Pompadour,
(*c*) Cleopatra.

I desire her to take Vicky for a walk; she is *blessée*, and much
time is spent in restoring her to calm.

Our Vicar's Wife — who has meantime been walking up and
down drawing-room in state of stress and agitation — says What
about asking somebody else? What about the Kellways? Why not
ring them up?

We immediately do so, and are light-heartedly told by Mary
Kellway that it *is* Fancy Dress, and she is going to wear her
Russian Peasant costume — absolutely genuine, brought by
sailor cousin from Moscow long years ago — but if in difficulties,
can she lend me anything? Reply incoherently to this kind offer,
as Our Vicar's Wife, now in uncontrollable agitation, makes it
impossible for me to collect my thoughts. Chaos prevails, when
Robert enters, is frenziedly appealed to by Our Vicar's Wife, and
says Oh, didn't he say so? one or two people *have* had 'Fancy
Dress' put on invitation cards, as Lady B.'s own house-party
intends to dress up, but no such suggestion has been made to
majority of guests.

Our Vicar's Wife and I agree at some length that, really,
nobody in the world *but* Lady B. would behave like this, and we
have very good minds not to go to her party. Robert and I then
arrange to take Our Vicar and his wife with us in car to party, she
is grateful and goes.

October 23rd
Party takes place. Black taffeta and Honiton lace look charming
and am not dissatisfied with general appearance, after extracting
two quite unmistakable grey hairs. Vicky goes so far as to say that
I look Lovely, but enquires shortly afterwards why old people so
often wear black — which discourages me.

Received by Lady B. in magnificent Eastern costume, with
pearls dripping all over her, and surrounded by bevy of equally

bejewelled friends. She smiles graciously and shakes hands without looking at any of us, and strange fancy crosses my mind that it would be agreeable to bestow on her sudden sharp shaking, and thus compel her to recognise existence of at least one of guests invited to her house. Am obliged, however, to curb this unhallowed impulse, and proceed quietly into vast drawing-room, at one end of which band is performing briskly on platform.

Our Vicar's Wife — violet net and garnets — recognises friends and takes Our Vicar away to speak to them. Robert is imperatively summoned by Lady B. — (Is she going to order him to take charge of cloak-room, or what?) — and I am greeted by an unpleasant-looking Hamlet, who suddenly turns out to be Miss Pankerton. Why, she asks accusingly, am I not in fancy dress? It would do me all the good in the world to give myself over to the Carnival spirit. It is what I *need*. I make enquiry for Jahsper — should never be surprised to hear he has come as Ophelia — but Miss P. replies that Jahsper is in Bloomsbury again. Bloomsbury can do nothing without Jahsper. I say, No, I suppose not, in order to avoid hearing any more about either Jahsper or Bloomsbury, and talk to Mary Kellway — who looks nice in Russian Peasant costume — and eventually dance with her husband. We see many of our neighbours, most of them not in fancy dress, and am astounded at unexpected sight of Blenkinsop's Cousin Maud, bounding round the room with short, stout partner, identified by Mary's husband as great hunting man.

Lady B.'s house-party, all in expensive disguises and looking highly superior, dance languidly with one another, and no introductions take place.

It later becomes part of Robert's duty to tell everyone that supper is ready, and we all flock to buffet in dining-room, and are given excellent sandwiches and unidentified form of cup. Lady B.'s expensive-looking house-party nowhere to be seen, and Robert tells me in gloomy aside that he thinks they are in the library, having champagne. I express charitable — and improbable — hope that it may poison them, to which Robert merely replies, Hush, not so loud — but should not be surprised to know that he agrees with me.

Final, and most unexpected, incident of the evening is when I come upon old Mrs Blenkinsop, all over black jet and wearing martyred expression, sitting in large armchair underneath platform, and exactly below energetic saxophone. She evidently has not the least idea how to account for her presence there, and saxophone prevents conversation, but can distinguish something about Maud, and not getting between young things and their pleasure, and reference to old Mrs B. not having very much longer to spend among us. I smile and nod my head, then feel that this may look unsympathetic, so frown and shake it, and am invited to dance by male Frobisher – who talks about old furniture and birds. House-party reappear, carrying balloons, which they distribute like buns at a School-feast, and party proceeds until midnight.

Band then bursts into Auld Lang Syne and Lady B. screams Come along, Come along, and all are directed to form a circle. Singular mêlée ensues, and I see old Mrs Blenkinsop swept from armchair and clutching Our Vicar with one hand and unknown young gentleman with the other. Our Vicar's Wife is holding hands with Miss Pankerton – whom she cannot endure – and looks distraught, and Robert is seized upon by massive stranger in scarlet, and Cousin Maud. Am horrified to realise that I am myself on one side clasping hand of particularly offensive young male specimen of house-party, and on the other that of Lady B. We all shuffle round to well-known strains, and sing For *Ole* Lang Syne, For *Ole* Lang Syne, over and over again, since no one appears to know any other words, and relief is general when this exercise is brought to a close.

Lady B., evidently fearing that we shall none of us know when she has had enough of us, then directs band to play National Anthem, which is done, and she receives our thanks and farewells.

Go home, and on looking at myself in the glass am much struck with undeniable fact that at the end of a party I do not look nearly as nice as I did at the beginning. Should like to think that this applies to every woman, but am not sure – and anyway, this thought ungenerous – like so many others.

Robert says, Why don't I get into Bed? I say, Because I am

writing my Diary. Robert replies, kindly but quite definitely, that In his opinion, That is Waste of Time.

I get into bed, and am confronted by Query: Can Robert be right?

Can only leave reply to Posterity.

The Mouchotte Diaries, 1940–1943

translated from the French by PHILIP JOHN STEAD

With the exception of the De Maisse Journal, all the extracts in this book are from English diaries. De Maisse, however, shows us English matters through a foreign eye – and so he is matched nearly four hundred years later by another Frenchman, René Mouchotte, who escaped to England to join the Free French forces during the Second World War. Mouchotte's wartime England has a flavour of its own.

When France capitulated to Hitler in June 1940, René Mouchotte was in Oran with the French air forces. He was one of those who contrived to purloin an aeroplane and make his escape. His diary is full of a wild patriotism, and his joy is boundless when he reaches England and is attached to the R.A.F. But the awful boredom of war, the delays, the posting to distant stations, the muddles and red tape that always confound such times, soon bring him to a state of raging frustration. Enthusiasm gives way to a bitter impatience, and as his friends are killed one by one, loneliness overtakes him, and he becomes deeply critical of England and the English . . .

1940

June 17th (Oran)
I have just heard the incredible news of the Capitulation on the radio. The thing is so inconceivable that you boggle at it, shattered, imagining all manner of things – a nightmare, a mistake,

enemy propaganda – to try and efface the horrible reality. The wretched radio completely shattered our over-strained nerves by sounding forth a ringing *Marseillaise*, the last call of a France that yesterday was free . . .

June 18th
France surrenders: her army, her navy, her air forces. General Noguès has just issued a rousing appeal to the troops in North Africa. A little hope. No other news. I haven't much faith. What will happen to England?

June 20th
. . . *I mean to go to England*. Since my country has rejected me as a combatant I will fight for her in spite of her and without her . . . Maybe in the future we shall know the truth about these painful days we live in. I want to be one of those who will chastise the men responsible for this war, for justice will inevitably be done. That same harsh justice will punish those who have now surrendered France while she could still fight, who abase themselves before the invader, and hand over, despite itself, the nation which was entrusted to them. The propaganda is filtering through even here; many are already turning their backs on England, their former ally, to blame her for the catastrophe. That is enough about that. It hurts too much. *I've got to get away* . . .

June 29th (Mouchotte with five others, including his friend, Charles Guérin, has commandeered a plane and they are over Gibraltar.)
. . . I concentrated hard. I put my flaps down rather soon; I prefer it that way. But it made me lose altitude too fast. A big burst from the engine; the plane was dragging; I was getting near the limit. I cut down the speed. In spite of my concentration on the landing, which went off very well, I noticed hundreds of English soldiers to right and left, running and waving wildly. But our eyes were also drawn to three or four French planes whose tricolour markings rejoiced our hearts. So others had preceded us? There were people here to expect us and greet us. Our nerves relaxed. Cries of joy filled the plane, all the louder because the

engines were running quietly . . . I opened a panel. There were welcoming shouts of 'Cheerio!' coming towards us . . . A crowd of soldiers surrounded us. There were handshakes, great smacks on the back. What big, kind fellows they were! They fought to offer us the first cigarette . . .

July 29th (in England)
. . . Women soldiers are extremely numerous in England and form a little army of their own, auxiliary to and in support of the big one in functions, uniform, ranks and communal life. In France one could not imagine the existence of such an army, probably because of the fear of ridicule. The spirit is so different here. These little soldiers each do their work with the utmost seriousness and astonishing conscientiousness. The first time I was saluted in the street in London was by a charming little blonde in uniform and nothing could have been more comical than to see her give the convulsive, snappy salute in the English style, turning her head towards me with imperturbable composure. We have just arrived at Old Sarum, three miles from Salisbury (my nerves are on edge with being unable to pronounce 'Soolsbeurré') . . . We got here last night and as from this morning we fly. It hasn't taken long. I was overjoyed to renew my acquaintance with the stick but the infernal throttle gives me endless trouble. The English, of course, do nothing like other people; on the road they drive on the left; in aviation they reverse the direction of the throttle . . .

August 5th
Charles and I have just been invited to a neighbouring lady's country home. A great reception was given in honour of the two Frenchmen. The two young daughters of the house did the honours. Introductions. All the fine flower of the district, girls in uniform and not in uniform, miniatures and caricatures, they all made inordinate efforts to give us the benefit of their three words of French, which they tore off at us with much laughter. Never, in so short a time, have I had to tell our story so often. In the end I knew the English sentences by heart, repeating the same words every time . . . My friend Charles has been getting by manfully

during his month here. His vocabulary increases on the average by a word and a half a week. I can make a faultless inventory of it: 'Yes. No. Darling. Very nice. I love you.' That is all . . .

October 10th (Northolt, with the Churchill Squadron)
. . . 'The job goes on all the time,' two Poles, who are leaving tomorrow for a rest, told me, 'you'll always be at readiness!' This Polish squadron has done a first-class job; in a month they have shot down 115 planes. This promises to be enormously interesting for us, but alas, what casualties! Nearly 50 per cent of their comrades have not returned from the battle . . .

October 11th
My first fighting mission: an event. Greatly excited. We took off, twenty-four of us, in three minutes: a record. There is always a layer of mist over London which nowadays almost completely hides the city and its suburbs. We soon went through this ceiling and at once found ourselves beneath an immensely blue sky. The radio was guiding us, probably to meet a German squadron making for England. In places we saw the ground, very small, for we were already at 22,000 feet. I was thinking hard. Memories, ideas rushed into my mind, while my hands were busy. I saw France. Far, far, very far off, the coast stood out clearly. Without wanting to be emotional, I abandoned myself to a feeling of great sadness and pity . . .

October 17th
Yesterday I had my first engagement with Messerschmidts, for an instant. I confess I didn't see very much, the Germans being well above us. I saw a Spitfire dive earthwards at a terrifying speed, trailing a cloud of black smoke after it. Poor lad! Another one. Up to us to carry on his work . . . Yesterday we flung our poor Hurricanes up desperately, throttles wide open. They wouldn't climb and we had the unpleasant impression of standing still. Appallingly unpleasant moments.

1941

January 24th

. . . I have rarely been more indignant than I was the other evening when a comrade told me of a conversation between two French Headquarters bureaucrats; they remarked that we have no Boche to our credit and spoke of us as 'debunked' . . . 'How many Jerries have you got?' That is the eternal question one is asked in London and elsewhere. Success in fighters is undoubtedly a question of courage, but no one will deny that luck has an equal share in it . . .

February 7th

Our flight went over France today, driving in as far as Arras. It was a black day for the squadron: three out of twelve planes did not return . . . Two friends, Perrin and Bouquillard, were shot down by the enemy. The former baled out; the latter, with many bullet wounds, landed in a field. In France they would have been mentioned in despatches; here they only just escaped being regarded as imbeciles. A delicate situation; sometimes it needs a lot of patience and courage not to let our morale go.

February 16th

A gale is blowing over the squadron. Nothing is going well. From orders badly given to planes deplorably maintained . . . No one would think this is a squadron on active service. The English mechanic repairs the part whose maintenance has been entrusted to him. *If he notices a defective part he has no orders to deal with, he will not touch it.* Apart from the periodical inspections, it is the pilot and the pilot alone who examines his plane each morning. If he finds anything wrong, however slight, a verbal order to the mechanic is not enough. He has to enter it in a book for the purpose. What a waste of time! How many human lives risked by negligence! . . .

May 10th (Charles Guérin, who escaped with Mouchotte, is lost. They are on convoy duty, fifty miles out to sea.)
... As we made for the coast, I advised him to bale out; we were at 4,000 feet. At last I heard his voice; he told me he could not get back. He was going to try and ditch near the convoy. My poor old Charles, if only you had listened to me! I kept as close to him as I could. He had opened the cockpit hood. His propeller was barely turning. In spite of that, a great cloud of white smoke completely enveloped the plane and must have blinded him. I talked to him to the very end, encouraging and advising him. Alas, when we were at 50 feet the most unforseeable thing happened. I can only explain it by the density of the glycol, which must have completely blinded Charles. He straightened his plane out, thinking he was at sea level, then with a savagely swift movement the plane lurched to starboard, skimmed the sea, turned over and vanished in less than a second ...

June 11th (Mouchotte's mother was in Occupied France.)
At last I have had two long letters from my mother. There are plenty of details. She seems quite reassured about me. I have told her, of course, in all my letters, that *I am an instructor*. Poor mother! It would kill her if she knew. French and English troops have gone into Syria. I ask myself bitterly what I am doing here in the heart of England while other comrades are fighting without respite and getting themselves killed.

October 30th
I am leaving 615 Squadron suddenly for Hornchurch. How many memories I leave behind me! Before my departure, General de Gaulle came to lunch with us. A great reception ... General de Gaulle came and chatted with us for a long time while photographers shot us. For the first time I have been near our Chief, *the great leader of Free France, to whom go out the hopes of all the true French in the world* ... I have always been glad to find that the General enjoys the unanimous respect and admiration of his colleagues. He rises above all mischievous rumours.

He is above all that. He loves his country and thinks of the end
to be attained . . .

1942

June 20th
We went with twelve Boston bombers in close escort over Le
Havre . . . shows of this kind, excellent for a novice, now leave
me quite cold . . . But what makes me *furious* today is to see how
clumsily the bombers have missed their target. Until now I have
always been a witness of their great accuracy. Obviously beginners,
completely bewildered by ack-ack. Coming in over Deauville,
they swung to port too soon to attack Le Havre from west to east
and arrived over their target at the end of their turn, still diving
. . . The results wrung a cry of indignation from me. A great part
of the bombs fell like a string of beads right along the principal
artery of the city. Heavy plumes of smoke came up; I thought
with horror of the wretches buried beneath the debris of their
houses, smashed by their friends of yesterday. Did they know
that the monsters who were ravaging their homes were protected
by Frenchmen? . . .

*By 1943 René Mouchotte had been promoted Commandant, had
formed a Free French fighter squadron known as 'Alsace', and had
been decorated by De Gaulle with the ribbon of the Légion d'Honneur.
He had become notorious as a daring flyer and fighter, but he was
growing desperately tired. He had taken part in more than 300
operations, totalling nearly two thousand flying hours. In July of that
year, he made this last entry in his diary, and the following month, on
the 27th August, he was shot down and died:*

And the sweeps go on, at a terrible pace . . . *I feel a pitiless weari-
ness from them.* It is useless for me to go to bed at 9.30 each night; I
feel my nerves wearing out, my temper deteriorating. The
smallest effort gets me out of breath; I have a crying need of rest,
were it even for forty-eight hours. I have not taken a week's leave
for two years . . . These last days I have tried to hold myself back,
fearfully anticipating the hard period of fighting ahead, for which
I shall need all my strength and fitness. I have therefore can-

celled all offensive work, confining myself to going nowhere but to the office ... But this three days relaxation has softened my nerves and my will. I am still as tired. Tomorrow I am flying again.

Recording Ruin

A. S. G. BUTLER

At the time of the Second World War a number of diaries were written and published, many about specialised aspects of the affair. Much was written about the civilian side of the conflict – about the fire service, about being an air raid warden or an ambulance driver. A. S. G. Butler, an architect, had the job of recording the damage to houses and property in the Borough of Chelsea, where he lived. He was also concerned with the business of fire-watching at St Paul's Cathedral. His experience of a fire raid makes a ghostly echo to Pepys, who wrote his account of London burning not quite three hundred years earlier.

1941

January 28th
Somebody said at lunch last Sunday that it sounds awfully dangerous, all this crawling about smashed-up houses. The remark reminded me so of what people thought our life was like at the front in the last conflict – how they imagined we were incessantly shelled, gassed and shot at, whereas we constantly dined, with three or four courses and in almost complete silence, in the very front line. So I explained that I do not go up broken staircases on purpose or cling to wobbling chimney-stacks often and only leap chasms when it is essential. I sometimes toboggan down a roof, but

M

always into a valley between that roof and the next, never just into space. After that, the lady was less perturbed – and much less impressed.

Sometimes I should like there to be more excitement in the work. It becomes so drearily dull going through seventeen houses all alike and all rather badly damaged in much the same way. It provokes serious and gloomy thoughts about the war – too gloomy often ...

Number 79b – that is the sort of number this house had – was uninhabited. Unlike most houses left empty, its front door was not locked because it had been split nearly in half by the adjoining explosion ... I kicked the door and it flew half-open and stuck – due to the fact that a mat, some floorboards, and a lot of plaster had created an obstacle. I got over this rather burstingly and went into the front room. The floor and most of the furniture were entirely covered with broken glass and powdered plaster, mixed. Bits of glass were sticking in the back wall of the room. One of them jagged my sleeve. The marble surrounding the fire was lying in a heap of soot from the chimney; and the overmantel had thrown its vases under the sofa opposite. All the middle of the ceiling had come down, including the usual heavy plaster orna-ment and converted gas bracket. They were in a heap on the table, mixed with harmonium music and cake. The thin partition-wall next the hall had burst open and knocked two fat stuffed birds off a shelf. The windows were voids with ragged edges and a lot of recent rain had blown through them, soaking the armchair which had since frozen stiff. Perhaps the dreariest things of all were the torn blue blinds, hanging in shreds with dried mud from the road on them. But, as so often happens, several pictures were still hanging – one even with its glass unbroken. I put it straight.

The kitchen and other back rooms were merely squalid. A horrid mixture of glass and broken chairs, old pots, unwashed dishes and a clock lying face downwards on a bowler hat. Plaster everywhere, in lumps and slabs and dirty powder. But the stairs were rather unusual. I suppose a tank in the roof had poured its water down them. Then, with the fierce frost of the last two days, the dying cascade had frozen and each step was a glacier. I fell

over twice going up, and a long icicle from the landing hit my
teeth because I failed to see it in the semi-darkness. It was not even
a clean icicle but a grubby-coloured one. And the bedrooms were
much the same. There was every sign of a very hurried exit.
Jumbled beds with frozen sheets, clothes and shoes and handbags
flung about. Half a perambulator lay by a window which had
fallen in frame and all — on top of it. The tipped-up little gas
cooker had a triumphant foot through a gramophone record. And
so on to the top, where the wrecking was worse. The roof was
nearly uncovered. Its slates were in the beds and the cistern
dangled by a feeble pipe above a squashed water-closet. Two
chimney-pots had crashed against the landing banisters and
pushed them over. The floors were frozen slush on the slimy lino.
The back wall was gone completely and the floors jutted and
drooped in space. A child's doll lay on the brink, with its head off
and its skirt blown up, showing its legs.

One develops a great pity for things. Just simple things made
by somebody and used for years by somebody else. I feel it now
and then more strongly than distress for people. Things are so
helpless and entirely innocent of all this rot. Then, in these
dismal houses, it is sad to think of the hours of good work
spent in creating their ugliness; but it is sadder to see even
that smashed up in a second. Perhaps one day when these infernal
wars are less frequent, we may feel more secure and have the
time and money to build houses at least worthy of our woods
and stones.

February 7th
It's curious how we get used to things — even the deadly howl of
the sirens. How we hated them at first! I cannot pretend that I
did not get the horrors the first time I heard them. I wonder if the
authorities chose on purpose their prepare-for-doom yell. Rather
insensitive of them, if so. But now it is quite different and means
just a little extra tension. In fact, when the warning came in King's
Road the other afternoon, people hardly paused or looked up or
stopped chatting about butter and lemons. They quite perk us
up — those sirens, when they go off in the night at St Paul's. They
give us old architects guarding it something to do, even if it is no

more than watching a distant fire from a bomb flare up and die
down again. Quite a blaze across the river, and reflected in the
water. But nothing very disastrous occurred.

April 17th

Well, we copped it last night. That is the verb, I think.
I've got worms in the head with all the noise, and my legs
won't quite walk. But otherwise am very well and rather
pleased.

It was, on the whole, grand. I was at St Paul's. The raid began
almost directly we had paraded, so that, as it waxed in fury, we
had only to slide into our emergency stations. Our job, as usual,
was to watch the roofs, patrolling for hours our various ambul-
atories. Nothing awful occurred for quite a long time. Only the
tumult of our own guns, breaking the roar of the enemy bombers,
seemed to rise in a slow crescendo. Where we were was really
very like being in a forward observation-post south of Arras
years ago, waiting to direct fire on the enemy, except that now
we were waiting to squirt water at him. On both occasions he
was invisible. In neither war have many people bashed each other
hand-to-hand ... Last night was just as much a battle as the
Somme ... It was a little boring for the first hour or two; and the
only relief was looking at the other buildings catching fire or
blowing up or – in a pause in the rumpus – smoking in a look-out
and chatting on our telephones. Everything worked very smoothly.
Then, some time between one and two in the morning, there
came a shower of incendiaries. Shower is the exact word – an
April shower proper to this month. It was short and very like the
preliminary whip of a hailstorm before a cold spring tempest in
the north. They rattled on our roofs with a tinny noise and we
went out after them ...

Several of the bombs, however, earned their living before being
killed. It takes more than a minute to reach some of our roofs –
up and down long ladders in the dark. So that, now and then, we
had to do more than merely quench the things. For they set light
to the oak boarding under the leads and this took some getting at
in places. We even had to use a hydrant once from underneath.
It made a small river down the stairs just as the Fire Brigade

came up to see us – I gather on an order from most exalted quarters. But there was nothing for them to do, probably to the disappointment of one who was a girl-driver, I expect. Nice for her to be able to say, all the same, that she was at St Paul's last night.

So it went on for hours. The roar of the enemy plunging about was terrific. They seemed to be whirling round the dome like silly screaming dragons. Looking out, I watched the furnaces near us and listened to the bells of the fire-engines clanging incessantly far below. A sudden flare-up looked like the Old Bailey bursting into a white sheet of light, then into red and orange flames darting at the crimson fog of smoke which enveloped us all. One became very tired with all the walking up and down short flights of steps and stumbling in the dark – all aggravated with the things one has to carry all the time, especially that blasted respirator. The view west was very lurid. I saw fire after fire in perspective and a big one towards Chelsea with, I expected, this house in it. I wondered if it was wholly wrecked and who had got out my old housekeeper and if James was whining for me under the ruins. And so became angry and really raged and thought that no form of government, no patriotism or country and no belief in anything whatever in the world justified this filthy insanity ... Then the heavy bomb came and pierced the transept roof. It blew up somewhere below, smashing the vault and the floor and our whole headquarters in the Crypt. Up in the dome area, we felt the shock of it nicely. St Paul's rocked. But only for an instant; then, quivering, settled down in its habitual majesty. We wondered if the Crypt patrol were killed. But they were not. Nobody was. Only our ordinary clothes, our latch-keys and our sandwiches, our wallets with our money and all the little cards and leaflets without which it is increasingly illegal to exist were buried in the debris ... We went on watching. Kind people struggled up endless stairs with tea. We blessed them and got all the news from below. Not a window left in the place. Even the iron frames wrenched out and flung about and a side wall rather bulged; but Wellington's monument was still intact and the Duke's horse still pranced, without a scratch, on top of it. Then, between four and five, it seemed our own 'planes were sweeping the sky. Not that we knew, but it sounded encouragingly like it. Until, in the blackened morning air and the harsh stink of frying offices, the All Clear came . .

Donald Crowhurst, 1932–1969

The last entry in this book is something of an epilogue. For years men have been writing down their experiences and their secret thoughts. Now they have other means, they have tape-recorders.

In 1968, Sir Francis Chichester having sailed single-handed round the world, it was inevitable that an attempt would be made to cap his achievement – by sailing round the world single-handed – *and* non-stop. *The Sunday Times* sponsored such a trip, and among the entrants was a man named Donald Crowhurst. Perhaps he was a man who needed to prove something to himself about himself. He chose a trimaran, *Teignmouth Electron,* for the venture and he set out, as it now seems, not very efficiently equipped. His wife loyally supported his ambitions and gave him all the encouragement he seemed to need.

Something went dreadfully wrong with Crowhurst's attempt. He was dogged by misfortune – failures of equipment and so on. At some point he realised he was not going to make it and he hit upon the idea of falsifying his log and *pretending* he had made the trip, sailing in, by careful timing, to collect the prize. He might easily have got away with it. But the responsibility of what he was doing, combined with the solitude and the dangers, unbalanced him. His boat was found drifting and empty. Whether he died by accident or design can only be judged by the words he left behind.

Some of those words are written diary-wise. Many are tape-recorded. It is difficult to decide which is the more intimate – a message written privately, or one spoken even more immediately, and with all the nuance of emphasis and inflection found in the living voice.

The Strange Voyage of Donald Crowhurst

NICHOLAS TOMALIN & RON HALL

1968

November 2nd

Earlier today porpoises came out to greet me. There were about 30 of them playing round the boat, accompanied by a mass of gulls. Sometimes as many as 6 pairs in a line (they seemed to prefer swimming in pairs) would jump on the starboard side and swim across the bows to port. All round the boat they were leaping and inspecting me! . . .

November 3rd

After reading *Ocean Passages* (*an Admiralty handbook*) I decided to make a westing. The weather would delight a clipper captain . . . A voice keeps saying 'Carozzo coming' and urges me to cut Ushant fine, but blow that, I'll sail this boat like a clipper. I may miss a few days, but it will be a lot safer, and anyway could just as easily save time if a West or South-West blow comes – as it very well may.

November 5th

Rachel's birthday. Happy birthday, Rachel. (*Rachel was his daughter.*) Hell of a morning for me, though. After putting up the main and making a course of SW, I was feeling pleased with myself when I noticed that bubbles were blowing out from the hatch when *Teignmouth Electron* rolled! To confirm my fears, the port bow float was shipping an awful lot more water than it should, as we were on the port tack. All the evidence was that the compartment was full of water.

I eased the ship to a course of West, and undid the butterfly nuts. The whole compartment was flooded, to deck level. I bailed out with a bucket, mopped up, and screwed down on a Sylgas fibreglass gasket. That should avoid further trouble. It was a long, exhausting job that took 3 hours, as I was shipping a good bit of water. The seas were 15 feet high, and the wind was about Force 7, so that as fast as I bailed, it came pouring back in!

I cursed the people who'd been kind enough to help me stow ship, and I cursed myself for a fool. I swore the boat was a toy fit only for the Broads or the pool at Earl's Court. But when I'd got the job done, eaten some curry and rice with an apple and some tea, I experienced the great satisfaction that something I'd been fearing had happened and had been dealt with. Now I must do all the other hatches. I looked into the port main hatch, and things seemed O K. I got out my vitamin pills. A whaler, French or Spanish, said hullo.

November 12*th*
Got up late again, having sailed 7 hours due north. This is not good enough. I must not allow myself to get so lazy. True it was blowing hard all yesterday and I was tired, but I am not here for a rest or to catch up sleep. It will take me 4 hours to make up the lost distance, a total waste of 11 hours – half a day. If I did that every day it would take over a year to finish. I MUST NOT ALLOW MYSELF TO BE LAZY.

November 13*th*
I disposed of an uneasy feeling about the date in the morning – I told myself 13 had never had an especially sinister significance for me. Today has had a sinister significance all right. Plugging away to westward in a southerly gale the cockpit hatch has been leaking and has flooded the engine compartment, electrics and Onan (*the generator*). Unless I can get the Onan to work I will have to think very seriously about the continuation of the project. With so much wrong with the boat in so many respects – it would perhaps be foolish or at any rate a subjective decision to continue. I will try to get the generator working, and think about the alternatives open to me.

November 15*th*
... Racked by the growing awareness that I must soon decide
whether or not I can go on in the face of the actual situation. What
a bloody awful decision – to chuck it in at this stage – what a
bloody awful decision! ...

*And, in fact, this was not quite the decision that he came to. Shortly
after this entry, part of a long assessment of his situation, he began on
what the authors of the book call the 'false log':*

December 6*th*
Set course further Southward. Have sailed 69 miles in about 24
hours, not really pushing but snug and safe at night – more or
less. Should be worth trying for 240 noon to noon ... Boom guy
parted, and jib pole folded up on shrouds – DAMN!

December 8*th*
01 10 If this wind holds I will do it! It seems as though it will
blow for ever! ...

December 9*th*
174 miles run today by the log, without any real effort!

*Crowhurst now began to vary his methods, sometimes writing his
impressions, sometimes recording, and often breaking into verse of one
sort and another. The time went on somehow, and on 23rd June –
'his last rational day' say his biographers – he concluded a tape with
the defiant words:*

I feel tremendously fit ... I feel as if I could realise all those
ambitions I nurtured as a boy like playing cricket for England. I
feel on top of the world, tremendously fit. My reflexes amaze me.
They're so fast, you know. I catch things almost before they
start falling. It's really very satisfying – I feel in tremendous
shape actually ... There is a danger that the way we live nowadays just poisons us with sitting down worrying. Worrying about
our nearest competitor in our level of the pyramid. The rat race!
All that plus the extremely unhealthy way of life. I'm sure we're

in terrible danger from it. And there's nothing like going back to
the sea, for getting rid of all the poisons, you know . . . The sea's
the way to get rid of them, I'm sure. I feel in tremendous shape . . .

*As his crisis mounted, Crowhurst's mind, increasingly confused, ex-
pressed itself in disjointed philosophies, and once again in writing:*

The shameful secret of God. The trick he used because the truth
would hurt too much. If it had been known before, the necessary
perfect shining instrument would not be what it is today.

The quick are quick, and the dead are dead. That is the judgment of God. I could not have endured the terrible anguish and
meaningless waiting, in fact.

There must be much we can learn from each other. Now at
last man has everything he needs to think like a cosmic being.

At the moment it must be true that I am the only man on earth
who realises what this means. It means I can make myself a cosmic
being, by my own efforts, but I have to hurry up and get on with
it before I die!

Man is forced to certain conclusions by virtue of his mistakes.

No machine can work without error!

The only trouble with man is that he takes life too seriously.

Eventually Donald Crowhurst wrote these lines:

11 15 00   It is the end of my
            my game the truth
            has been revealed and it will
            be done as my family require me
            to do it

11 17 00   It is the time for your
            move to begin

            I have no need to prolong
            the game

It has been a good game that
must be ended at the
I will play this game when
I choose I will resign the
game 11 20 40 There is
no reason for harmful

These are his last words.

ACKNOWLEDGEMENTS

The Editor and Publishers are indebted to the following for the use of copyright material: Mr R. A. Jones, Mr G. B. Harrison, and David Higham Associates Ltd for extracts from *The De Maisse Journal of 1597*, published by The Nonesuch Press; Longman Group Limited for extracts from *Lord Macartney's China Journal 1793–1794*, edited by J. L. Cranmer Byng; J. M. Dent & Sons Ltd for extracts from *Fanny Burney's Diary* reproduced from the Everyman's Library text; Oxford University Press for extracts from the *Journals of Dorothy Wordsworth*, edited by Mary Moorman, with an introduction by Helen Darbishire, published in 1971; Oxford University Press for extracts from *The Journal of Gideon Mantell 1818–1852*, edited by E. Cecil Curwen; Sidgwick & Jackson Ltd for extracts from *Marjory Fleming's Journals 1809–1811*; Hodder & Stoughton Ltd for extracts from *A Norfolk Diary 1850–1888* by Richard Armstrong; Mr F. R. Fletcher and Jonathan Cape Ltd for extracts from *Kilvert's Diary* edited by William Plomer; George Allen & Unwin Ltd for extracts from *The Story of My Life* by Augustus Hare; Victor Gollancz Ltd for extracts from *The Diary of Ivy Jacquier 1907–1926*; William Heinemann Ltd for extracts from *Medicine and Duty* by Harold Dearden; Mrs Dorothy Cheston Bennett and Penguin Books Ltd for extracts from *The Journals of Arnold Bennett 1896–1929*, edited by Dorothy Cheston Bennett; Quentin Bell, Angelica Garnett and The Hogarth Press for extracts from *A Writer's Diary 1918–1941* by Virginia Woolf; A. D. Peters & Company for extracts from *Diary of a Provincial Lady* by E. M. Delafield, published by Macmillan & Co. Ltd; Staples Press, Ltd for extracts from *The Mouchotte Diaries 1940–1943*, translated by Philip John Steed; the Executors of the Estate of the late A. S. G. Butler for extracts from *Recording Ruin*, published by Constable & Co. Ltd; Hodder & Stoughton Ltd for extracts from *The Strange Voyage of Donald Crowhurst* by Nicholas Tomalin and Ron Hall.